Wanting
to be
Loved

a spiritual perspective
on love, sex and relationships

Neroli Duffy
with Peter Duffy

BASED ON THE TEACHINGS OF
Elizabeth Clare Prophet

DARJEELING PRESS
Emigrant, Montana

Contents

Contents

Wanting to Be Loved

The impetus for me to compile a book on love, sex and relationships came from a lively discussion about dating with a group of teenage girls one summer evening. These young women were seeking to avoid the pitfalls of relationships and wanted to find a higher approach to love.

We talked about love, dating, marriage, finding the right partner in life, their concerns about AIDS and sexually transmitted diseases, and the reasons to wait until they were married to be sexually active. All too soon our time together was over, and I found myself wishing that I had a little book to give them that answered the many questions that we had not had time to talk about.

I left our conversation impressed with their sincerity and desire for true love. I was also aware of the challenges on the road that lay ahead of them.

The next day I happened to meet another teen, who shared with me her recipe for a happy life: someone to love and be loved by, something to do, and something to look forward to. As she turned to leave, she said to me, "We all just want to be loved." Her words stayed with me—*wanting to be loved*.

Most of us have a need to relate to at least one other individual in a very personal and intimate way. We all want to be loved. Yet all around us, we see marriages and relationships struggling as people desperately search for love and fail to find it. We see many people accepting less, often settling for sex when what they are really looking for is love. When people do settle for less, it is the cause of much grief and many backward steps on the path of life.

It is my hope that the concepts presented here will give hope that it is possible to find true love, that this is something to aim for, something that can be achieved. There is no need to settle for something less.

I pray that this message might inspire many to seek and find the love that they have always known is waiting for them—perhaps just around the next bend in the road of life.

Introduction

Who we love and why we love can have a profound effect on the course of our lives. As a doctor and a minister, I have observed the choices many people have made in their lives, loves and relationships. I have also observed these choices in my own life—and this is where I will begin.

From an early age, I always believed there was one special person for me. As I look back, it seems that I was always looking for love, and the search for the beloved was a compelling urge within me from a very early age. I remember being on the playground at school looking at the faces of the little boys there, wondering, as I searched for that special pair of eyes, "Is this the one? Is this the one?"

I was fortunate to have parents who taught me about the spiritual nature of love. They not only gave me their own example of a loving relationship, but their explanation of what happens spiritually in relationships helped me in the choices that I was to make in life.

My father had been a soldier in the Pacific in World War II and was later a policeman. He had seen much in the course of his work, and he tried to pass on to me some of the lessons he had learned. I will never forget a conversation one evening at dusk as we drove through Fremantle, Western Australia, the city in which I was born. I was a sixteen-year-old high school student.

My dad and I would often go to our favorite trattoria to sit outside with a cappuccino and watch the world go by. Sometimes we would walk through the streets up by the Fremantle museum. But this time, we drove right past our favorite areas to a more seedy part of town. My dad wanted to show me where the prostitutes lived and worked.

I never really knew this part of Fremantle existed. It is now a trendy area with shops and boutiques, but in those days it was the back streets of the old seaport. I felt as if we were passing into another world. As we drove past buildings that functioned as brothels, I saw young, middle-aged and even older women leaning out of the windows and against the doors, and my heart went out to them. Although some were dressed up and wore makeup, it was not hard to see the pain in their eyes and their lethargy of spirit. Some looked hardened. I felt a hostility from some of them that made me glad to be safe in the car with my father.

He explained to me that these women looked tired and old before their time because they had spent the light in their auras. Light is intended to be stored in the spiritual centers in the body, and we only have so much light available to us. When we spend that light in the misuse of sexual energy, it's gone.

My father explained that the bonds of marriage form a protective circle for the union of man and woman and the exchange of sexual energy. He also said that these women were not only losing their own life-energy, they also took inside of themselves a little bit of everyone with whom they slept. More than that, they also took in a little of everyone that those people had slept with. Over time, this would become a great burden to them, not only in their physical bodies, but also in their emotions, their mental worlds and in their spiritual beings.

As you can imagine, this visit made a profound impression on an innocent sixteen-year-old.

Ten years later, as a medical doctor working in a mining town in Western Australia, I treated some of the prostitutes who came to the practice where I worked. I had great compassion for them. Their lives were difficult and there were many reasons why they had ended up in this life. Many felt they had no alternative. And once again, I had the opportunity to observe the effects of the choices they made.

It wasn't just the venereal disease and the lifestyle that went with their profession, although these were bad enough. When I compared their physical appearance with the age on their medical charts, I was astounded. They looked so much older than their years.

I remember when I asked one of these women what she did for a living, not knowing her occupation. She answered in a matter-of-fact way, "I'm a worker." When I realized that she was a sex worker, it struck me as such a sad statement of her life. She did not "make love"—she "worked." Her life was so far from the true love she really wanted.

In the course of my medical practice and later in my years as a minister, I have been privileged to have many men and women share their stories of love and relationships with me. Some of the stories were very sad, and I could do little but offer support.

I remember a young teenager, a virgin. After one night of love, she now has genital herpes. I have to break this news to her and tell her that there is no cure. She will have to live with this painful and debilitating condition for the rest of her life. She cries on my shoulder, feeling guilty and at the same time so hurt because life seems so unfair.

Another woman in her early thirties suffers depression when she learns that the man she loved and expected to marry had been unfaithful to her. She weeps as she comes to me for a series of tests for a variety of sexually transmitted diseases, trying to come to grips with the fact that he had not one but many lovers.

A man in his mid-forties has lost his wife to cancer and must now face raising his children alone, wondering how he is ever going to face life without his partner by his side. He later has the good fortune to meet and fall in love with a wonderful woman who knows she can never replace his wife, but who loves him and cares for his children, who need a mother.

I can still see their faces and remember their stories. And I remember the lessons I learned from their lives.

Not all of the stories were sad. Many had joyful and happy lives.

I remember visiting one woman in her seventies the night before her surgery. She spoke of what it was like to be in love. She had been happily married for many years and was now an elderly widow, but the memory of that love was as fresh as if it were yesterday. As she spoke, it seemed to light up her whole face, giving her a youthful glow.

As an anesthetist, I was in a hurry to get everything done in preparation for the next day's surgical list, and I had several other patients to see. But I could not help but linger by her bed as she spoke about the love of her life. At the time, I was dating a young man. He was nice enough, a fellow doctor. On paper, it looked like a good match, but the spark was not there. I knew I did not want to marry him. I was seeking love and not finding it, wondering if there would ever be someone for me.

So I asked my patient, "How did you know that he was the right one?" She intuited the reason for my question and answered, "Oh, when the time comes, you'll know."

I am not sure I believed her then, even though I really wanted to. True love seemed to be something so far away. Although I had a wonderful career and loved my work, I was lonely and unfulfilled. I had an inner knowing that there was someone I was meant to be with. But how to find him?

It was about this time that I came upon Elizabeth Clare Prophet and her spiritual perspective on love, marriage and relationships. As I read her writings, my eyes were opened to a wider world of love, more than just the human love between man and woman, as important as that love may be. She spoke about the love of God for the soul, the love of the Higher Self, and the mysteries of divine love at the heart of the spiritual path.

As I heard all this, my heart leaped and I was eager to know more. I sent to America for an audio album on twin flames and soul mates. When it arrived, eight weeks later, I sat down and listened to it right away. My soul was hungry for a wisdom that might lift my burdens. I loved that album and played it over and over until I almost knew it by heart. The message was sweet in my mouth, as the Bible says, but also "bitter in the belly,"[1] because it meant making changes in my life and taking personal accountability.

One thing was very different. Now I knew who I had been looking for all those years. It was the one I had met in the heaven-world before this life. I knew he was out there, somewhere, and that one day I would meet him. I also knew I would have to be patient.

It seemed like I waited a long time. We finally found each other when we were in our thirties. The love we now share was well worth the wait.

I truly believe that a spiritual understanding of love can shed light on the choices we make in life. However, this knowledge does come with a price. You will find, as I did, that there are consequences to our choices, that we have accountability for our actions. And in the end, if we want the perfect love, we may have to make some sacrifices.

However, these sacrifices seem insignificant when we find the blessing of real love and the joy of fulfilling our purpose in life.

1
True Love

Love is our true destiny. We do not find the meaning of life by ourselves alone—we find it with another.

THOMAS MERTON

It All Begins in Heaven

Y ou've heard the phrase "a marriage made in heaven." Well, it's true. There are many marriages made in heaven. The most ancient and memorable is the union of God as Father and God as Mother.

In fact, we are all born of the union of the love of the Father-Mother God. This is the divine love that produced the creation of our own soul and that of our twin flame, the other half of the divine whole that we are. Together we reflect the consciousness of the Father-Mother God in loving union and the wholeness of that love.

There are many marriages on earth that were first made in heaven, planned by the angels and our Higher Selves—either twin flames or other souls brought together in commemoration of that inner polarity. But not every earthly marriage is a reflection of a heavenly one.

When we were in the heaven-world, before we entered these bodies we now wear, we could see clearly. We reviewed our life-to-be with heavenly guides. We understood the choices we would be given, the tests life would bring and our higher purpose on earth. If a relationship was part of our plan, we met with the Higher Self of the person who was destined to be our partner in this life. We saw our life plan—the mission we were created to fulfill, the children we would bring forth, the work we would do together and the love we would share.

But now that we have arrived down here on earth, it is somehow not so easy. Most of us do not remember what we agreed to in heaven, and the inner knowledge becomes clouded over with the veils of forgetfulness. We are left with a dim recall of some kind of plan and a sense of longing at the soul level. We yearn to meet others with whom we can connect, perhaps even the very ones we knew in the heaven-world before we entered life on earth.

In the meantime, our souls face many tests. Life can be hard, true love can seem unattainable, and there are many distractions that can divert us from the path we were intended to take. At times like this, it helps if we remember that *there is a plan.*

The Alchemy of Love

Love takes many forms. When we speak of love, we often think first of the love between man and woman, between husband and wife. But think of love in a broader sense. There is also the love within the family, the love of the master for the disciple, the love of God for his children, the love of the angels and masters of light for mankind, the love of the Higher Self for the lesser self that is in the state of becoming.

Love is the glue that holds families and communities and nations together. It is as if the whole experience that is life on earth is suspended between strands of love in all of its beautiful manifestations. Love really does make the world go round—and the love between a man and a woman is part of this love.

The world suffers from a lack of love. All problems, whether personal or planetary in scope, can ultimately be distilled to this single issue. What are terrorism, crime or war but an absence of love between brother and brother? What is child abuse but an absence of the love of the parent for the child?

In contrast, think of those who love without reserve, who risk their lives to rescue a child in danger, or those who put their own problems aside to help a neighbor in the aftermath of a flood or tornado. These are demonstrating a Christ-like love.

We all impact the world around us. Our lives and the love we share can touch every other soul on earth, whether we know it or not. Our love (or lack of it) may have even more far-reaching consequences than we realize. Love can literally change a world.

The Tibetan Master, Djwal Kul, tells a story of such a love:

There lived by the sea a gentle soul who was a miller. He and his wife served together to grind the grain for the people of their town. And it came to pass that in all the land there were no communities where so much happiness reigned as there. Their countrymen marveled and wondered, for they recognized that something unusual must have happened to make the members of this community so singularly wise and happy. And although the townsfolk themselves were born, grew up, matured to adulthood and passed from the screen of life within the community, never in all of their living were they able to understand the mystery.

Tonight I shall draw aside the curtain and tell you what made the people of this community so happy and prosperous, so joyous and wise.

It was the service of the miller and his wife and the love they put into the flour. For this love was carried home in sacks of flour on the backs of those who patronized their mill and was then baked into their bread. At every meal the regenerative power of love from the miller and his wife was radiated around the table, and it entered their physical bodies as they partook of the bread. Thus, like radioactive power, the energy of this vibrant love from the miller and his wife was spread throughout the community.

The neighbors did not know the reason for their happiness, and none of the people were ever able to discover it. For sometimes—although they live side by side—mankind are unable to pry the most simple secrets about one another.[1]

Does the story of the miller and his wife seem like a fable? Perhaps it does in this cynical era. But it is the allegorical story of twin flames sharing God's love with the world.

It can also be the story of you and your twin flame.

First, Look Within

n looking for love, one of the most important lessons we learn is that the search begins within. Instead of looking only outside of ourselves for love, we can first concentrate on magnifying the love that is already in each of us as the individual God-flame.

This is our own point of contact with the greatest source of love, which is God. If we want to have true love in our lives, how better to find it than to tie in to that universal source? So we find that if we put God first in life, all other things will begin to fall into place, and the light and love we find within will become a magnet for the perfect love without.

Unfortunately, the love we hold for God does not always reflect the love God holds for us. The unrelenting pursuit of the soul by a loving God is the theme of the poem "The Hound of Heaven," by Francis Thompson.

> I fled Him, down the nights and down the days;
> I fled Him, down the arches of the years;
> I fled Him, down the labyrinthine ways
> Of my own mind; and in the mist of tears
> I hid from Him....

At different points throughout the journey of life, the soul hears the voice of God speaking the lessons of experience of those who do not allow the love of God to enter:

"Lo! naught contents thee, who content'st not Me!...
Lo, all things fly thee, for thou fliest Me!"

The final stanzas move inexorably toward the capture as God unveils to the soul his ever-present love:

"Alack, thou knowest not
How little worthy of any love thou art!
Whom wilt thou find to love ignoble thee
Save Me, save only Me?
All which I took from thee I did but take,
Not for thy harms,
But just that thou might'st seek it in My arms....

"Ah, fondest, blindest, weakest,
I am He Whom thou seekest!
Thou dravest [drove] love from thee,
        who dravest Me."

Unknowing, the soul often flees from God—and thus from love itself. For God is love, and the world suffers from a lack of love through not receiving the greatest love of all.

The great yogi Paramahansa Yogananda used to recite this poem in his rich and resonant voice, seeking to inspire in his students the same great love that he felt for God. A yogi and a renunciate who had taken monastic vows, he never married, but he had much to teach about love and even about the love of man and woman. He taught that marriage is intended to be a reflection of the love between the soul and God, the lover and the Beloved. The soul reincarnates again and again until the lessons of love are learned.

Sometimes people have a sense of God as being somehow possessive in his love of us—that if we love him, he will not allow us to have any other loves in our life. But this is not so. God wants us to love him and to also have loving relationships that will further our spiritual growth and through which he can express his love in the world. Like a loving parent, God wants to see his children happy in life and love. That is one reason why God created man and woman.

In order to understand this love, we need to take a closer look at the love that is found in three kinds of relationships— twin flames, soul mates and relationships of karma. Each is unique in its own way, and each is an essential point of our understanding of the loves and relationships that exist in the world.

But first, let's look at karma and reincarnation, for like it or not, karma affects us all and influences all of these relationships.

The Law of Return

Karma is the law of cause and effect—as we sow, so shall we reap. All of life is energy. All that we think, feel and do has results in the world in which we live, and what we send out to others returns to us. And by the law of attraction, it gathers more of its kind as it returns.

If we send out love and kindness, then love and kindness will return to us. If we engage in harmful or unkind behavior, that negative energy also returns to us to be balanced. There is no injustice in the universe; what we send out comes back to us—with interest. Sometimes it comes back quickly, sometimes it takes a longer time to return.

Each day we have the opportunity to make positive or negative karma—through good or bad thoughts, feelings, actions and words. The choice is ours alone. And each day we have an account to settle in the ledger of life. Are we in the black or in the red at the end of that day?

We make good karma by helping and serving others, by giving love and compassion and sending out peaceful thoughts, by taking right steps and taking a stand for truth, and by defending life—especially when life is helpless.

We make bad karma when we send out harmful thoughts and feelings, when we do harmful and unkind things, when we use unkind and hurtful words. We can also make negative karma by acts of omission—when we don't speak up or act when we should act, when we let an opportunity for good pass us by.

We all have debts to life or we would not be here on earth. Those debts cry out to be balanced, and most take love to balance them. Some debts require us to love and serve another person in a very personal way, and our soul knows why we love. We are called by our Higher Self to balance the karma of unloving behavior by loving another from the depths of our heart and soul.

As we seek to balance our karma and learn the meaning of true love, we exercise God's gift of free will. By free will, we choose to love. God never denies us our free will. He does not interfere with our choices, unless we ask. God wants us to experience the consequences of our decisions, for that is how we learn.

In the past—in this or prior lives—we may have misused the light and energy he has given us, and in order to be entrusted with greater light and energy, we must prove that we will be responsible and use it constructively. We must prove that we will give love and not hatred.

The story of Kara and Robert* illustrates a tie of karma that led to marriage and the opportunity to balance that karma through love. It also illustrates the choices we have through free will.

When Kara met Robert, she was magnetically drawn to him, and at the same time there was something about him that made her very uncomfortable. She was wary, but she knew that Robert loved her and she loved him. They believed in the same

* All the stories in this book are true. The names of the individuals and some details have been changed to protect the privacy of those who shared their stories with me.

things and shared their faith. This seemed to be enough for her to be able to overcome her concerns.

They married and had three children in quick succession, but gradually she began to realize that Robert had neither the emotional nor mental stability that she brought to the marriage. He repeatedly made unwise choices, used drugs without her knowledge, was unfaithful and then wanted to return to her. He would fly into a rage at the least provocation or none at all. He was eventually diagnosed with bipolar disorder.

They tried again and again to make the marriage work, but she finally realized that he would never change. She could see that this marriage was not going to last. She knew she had to divorce him, salvage what she could of her life and rebuild her family as best she could. So that is what she did. As they divorced he sought custody of the children, denounced the spiritual path that they once shared, and started using drugs openly in front of their children. The whole situation turned into a nightmare.

While Kara was seeking to make sense of this marriage and why it had gone so wrong, she had a recall which helped her to understand the ties that had brought them together and the debt that they owed one another. Her recall was that Robert had murdered her in a past life. She also understood that taking a life brought about intense karmic ties and a karmic debt to Robert which needed to be paid, sometime, somewhere.

She did not know what other karma there was between them or how far back it went, but in this present life she greatly desired to help his soul so that they could both be free of the ties that bound them. She knew that this was a worthy desire, as he was also loved of God—as all souls are. She also recalled being shown by angel advisors that it was not likely that he would respond to her love. She did not have to marry him to balance her karma, but she could do so if she wanted to.

Does Kara regret her choice to marry Robert?

She would answer no, even though she realizes that if she had to do it over again, she might not make the choice to enter into this karmic marriage. But she does not dwell on the past. Together they brought three beautiful children into the world, and she balanced her karma with Robert. She is not bitter and she is wiser now. More importantly, she is free.

Situations of negative karma can be very challenging, but they can also be a blessing if we can learn and grow from the lessons they bring. Through a great deal of pain, Kara learned the lesson that both love and hatred are created out of the only energy there is—God's energy. It is our choice to use that energy to love or to hate. Whatever we decide, that energy goes out into the world around us, not just to the person we send it to. It gathers more of its kind, and it returns to our doorstep as the blessing of positive or negative karma.

As the miller and his wife silently communicated their love to their community, so you and your twin flame or soul mate or karmic partner influence countless lives around you through your thoughts, feelings and actions, which broadcast their energy out into the world. Every day you have an opportunity to make bad karma or good karma—to place a burden upon life or to assist life—either by recycling the negative energy of your past karma coming to the surface or by recognizing this energy as a challenge to your harmony and love and transforming it.

The Quest for Wholeness

The quest for love—and for the perfect partner in life—is really the quest for wholeness. We are seeking the other half of the whole, the part of us that we know exists somewhere in the cosmos.

Each of us yearns to reunite with our twin flame, the one who was created with us in the beginning. We ask ourselves, "Why is it that we are not together? How did we get separated from each other? How can we find each other again?"

Let's go back to the beginning of the story.

Aeons ago you and your twin flame stood before the Father-Mother God and volunteered to take embodiment to bring God's love to earth. The original plan was to go through a series of incarnations on earth and then to return to the heart of God.

While on earth, however, we fell from the state of perfection by misusing God's light. We made karma. Separated vibrationally from our Higher Self, we soon became separated from our twin flame. We remained apart in subsequent lifetimes due to our inharmony, fear and mistrust. Each lifetime apart from our twin flame was spent either creating negative karma, thus widening the gulf between us, or balancing some of the karma that stood in the way of our reunion.

Now is the time, at the turning of ages, when people are

again seeking to contact their twin flames. There is great opportunity to balance karma, to reconnect with one's twin flame, to return to the heart of God. The search for the twin flame is prompted by our Higher Self, but the search is often misunderstood by the outer mind.

Twin flames share a unique mission, but this does not necessarily mean they are intended to be together physically in this lifetime. Sometimes when people learn that they share a mission with their twin flame, they begin an outer search for that one special soul, just as I did. Unfortunately, this is almost always a detour on the spiritual path, because it is our relationship to God and our Higher Self that holds the key to fulfilling our mission and finding and becoming one with our twin flame.

No matter how separated by time and space, you are always connected with your twin flame at the innermost levels of being.

Because both you and your twin flame share the same blueprint of identity—like the design of a snowflake, unique in all of cosmos—whatever energy you send forth is imprinted with that specific pattern. According to the law of attraction, all energy you release also cycles to your twin flame, either hindering or helping that one on the path to wholeness.

When you send forth love or hope, these qualities will uplift your twin flame. If you are burdened with frustration or hatred, your twin flame will likewise feel the weight of these inharmonious feelings.

In the same way, wherever your twin flame is, whatever his or her state of consciousness is, can greatly influence your own path of life. Sometimes the inexplicable joys or depressions you feel are the moods of your other half registering on your own consciousness.

No matter how separated by time and space, you are always connected with your twin flame at the innermost levels of being. If you raise your own consciousness, you will also help your other half. The more you balance the karma that has separated you, the closer you will be in vibration. As you pursue your spiritual path, the inner tie will grow stronger and more tangible— and the outer meeting will also come to pass as it is ordained.

Recognizing Your Twin Flame

n his book *The Prophet*, Kahlil Gibran captures the essence of the relationship of twin flames:

> You were born together, and together you shall be
> forevermore.
> You shall be together when the white wings of death
> scatter your days.
> Aye, you shall be together even in the silent memory of
> God.

The relationship of twin flames is eternal. It is always there. It is not something you have to find on the outer. It is something you attune with on the inner. If you make that inner attunement, the outer connection and recognition may follow. If you don't have the inner attunement, you might be standing right next to your twin flame and never know it.

Recognition of the twin flame is an inner knowing—the knowledge of the soul. The outer senses will not tell you. Nor can you tell twin flames by appearance or astrology or common interests. Twin flames do not necessarily look alike. Twin flames may have very different habit patterns and personalities, divergent interests or "incompatible" astrology.

You cannot even tell a twin flame by the feelings of attraction. Sometimes twin flames may not even like each other when they meet. During lifetimes together, discord between them may have created much karma and lingering animosity; in lifetimes apart they may have evolved in very different ways. Ultimately it is karma that separates twin flames and causes them not to recognize one another. This karma can only be dissolved by spiritual work, balancing the karma and striving on the path so that the underlying love can be revealed.

What should you do if you meet someone you feel may be your twin flame? How do you know if you should be together?

Instead of looking for outer signs, it is better to still the senses and come apart for a while. Let your inner knowing tell you. Enter a period of aloneness. Fast and pray. Ask God to show you the rightness or wrongness of the relationship. And do not move until you are sure. As the saying goes, "Don't move until an elephant steps on your foot!"

The difference between inner and outer recognition is seen in this story of twin flames who did find one another, despite their karma. When Eleanor and Walter first met, there was no outstanding attraction. Eleanor was fifteen years older than Walter. He was interested in another woman at the time. Several years later the circumstances of life placed them side by side, working in the same department in a medium-sized business.

Little irritations and annoyances began to crop up between them. One day they were working on a project together and they began to disagree about how it should be done. An intense dislike for this man surfaced in Eleanor, and she said to herself, "I wouldn't marry Walter if he was the last man on earth!"

Immediately she heard her inner voice saying, "O yeah?

Well, look again. He is your twin flame." The realization was shocking at first. Walter, her twin flame? She did not say anything to him, but she prayed about it.

Eleanor realized that if they were twin flames, there must be considerable karma between them, and she began to work on this spiritually. She used the spiritual light known as the violet flame to dissolve and transmute that negative karma. (We will talk about the violet flame later in this book.) She tried to let go of her feelings of irritation and annoyance and keep her harmony when they were working together so as not to make any new karma.

Over a period of several years, Walter came to respect her. Gradually the differences between them began to dissolve. As the anger and irritation were transmuted, they found that despite their differences, they fell in love. By and by they received the outer confirmation of their inner intuition. Walter and Eleanor were married and adopted three children. Their life is full and they are grateful to be together.

They came to realize that they had been separated for many lifetimes by allowing discord to occur between them. The universe brought them together for another opportunity to balance their karma and serve together. They now strive to put aside the differences that come up from day to day. After being apart for so long, they do not want to let anything come between them in this round.

The Love of Twin Flames

When people learn of the concept of twin flames, they sometimes think, "If only my twin flame were beside me, all would be well." This is what I thought when I first found out about twin flames. But it is an illusion to assume that all problems will be resolved by meeting your twin flame.

While many twin flames have been reunited and live happily together, there are some who have met in this life and the encounter has not resulted in a lasting love. They fell in love, but then allowed forces and momentums of negativity to overwhelm that love. Some became involved in alcohol or drugs, preferring other loves to the pure love of twin flames. Some allowed explosions of anger and argument that are fraught with the creation of karma. Finally they went their separate ways, driven apart by discord and inharmony, while the angels in heaven wept for a lost opportunity.

One couple who were twin flames first met in their thirties. Phillip was a born-again Christian. Regina followed a spiritual path that honored the religions of both East and West. She knew right away that they were twin flames; he took longer to realize it. They fell in love, got married and began to work through their karma.

But even though they loved each other deeply and were twin

flames, it seemed that Phillip could not settle comfortably into the relationship. His job kept him on the road for much of the time and he started having casual sexual encounters, which broke Regina's heart. How could he not love her as she loved him?

They began to drift apart, and nothing Regina did or said seemed to make a difference or have an impact on him. Eventually they separated and divorced.

This story is a reminder that finding one's twin flame does not answer all of life's needs. Free will reigns supreme. Both parties have to want the same things and be willing to make some sacrifices or compromises for the sake of a higher love.

We must also realize that our twin flame may not be available to enter into a relationship with us in this life or at this time. The twin flame may already be married, may be much younger or older than us, or may not be in embodiment at all.

In fact, if an outer relationship between twin flames is not going to serve a higher purpose, then it may not be destined in this life. In these cases the Higher Self often does not reveal to the outer mind what the soul knows at a subconscious level—a knowledge that might lead to a detour from the individuals' life plans.

Sometimes, however, the outer awareness is there along with the inner connection, even while the individuals know that they have different roles they are destined to play.

Betty and Brian were both in their sixties when they met. She had been happily married for more than thirty years. A mother and grandmother, she had pursued a spiritual path for many years and soon recognized Brian as her other half when he walked into a study group that she held in her home.

Betty knew the importance of not making any new karma with her twin flame, and she did not say anything about her soul recognition. She treated Brian the same way as she treated everyone else in the group, and no one suspected that there was anything special between them.

Over time, however, Brian also became aware of the connection. He implored her to leave her husband and marry him, but Betty knew it was not a part of their divine plan to marry in this life. She loved Brian deeply, but she was not in love with him in the romantic sense.

Betty had a quiet, thoughtful nature. Brian was impulsive and outgoing. Betty drew a loving but firm boundary around their relationship. She continued to help Brian on his own spiritual journey, but she would not consider leaving her husband, whom she loved, nor would she forsake their vows and the family they had built together.

Twin flames do not necessarily need to be together physically in order to fulfill their joint mission. The inner tie and the spiritual connection in itself can be a great source of strength as they serve in different fields.

Several years later, Brian passed on suddenly of a stroke, partly because he did not take care of his rising blood pressure. Betty prayed for him after his passing, asking for him to be taken by the angels to his rightful place in preparation for the next steps on his spiritual journey. Within a year her granddaughter gave birth to a baby boy, whom she recognized by intuition as the reincarnation of her twin flame. She was able to pray for him and participate in his care and upbringing.

One day she was traveling with her great-grandson in the car. He was only three or four years old, but he was able to let her know that he recalled the times when he had known her in a past life. He kissed her and thanked her. She told him it would be best if he did not share this knowledge with others in the family, since they would not understand. Betty also kept this secret until she confided in me as a minister.

She told me that she saw many signs that this was the soul of Brian in a much younger body. He had the same outgoing personality, and she was happy to see that he was learning at an early age to curb his impulsive nature.

When Betty was in her seventies, her great-grandson would visit her and I would see Betty walking hand in hand with this eight-year-old boy. It was a joy to behold the pure love between these souls, and it was clear that once again it was not the divine plan for a romantic involvement in this life.

Ten years later Betty passed on. Perhaps she is waiting for her twin flame to fulfill his own life here below and return to her in the octaves of light. He has the support of a loving and caring family who understand spiritual matters, and he has a twin flame in heaven who is supporting him and praying for him.

Twin flames do not necessarily need to be together physically in order to fulfill their joint mission. The inner tie and the spiritual connection in itself can be a great source of strength as they serve in different fields. Sometimes there is the opportunity for only a brief time together, as in the case of these two souls—a source of inspiration that can set the sail for a lifetime's service.

Twin flames do not have to meet to balance karma. You can balance karma with your twin flame wherever that one is, in other octaves or at your side. We balance karma through loving relationships with all whom God sends to us, through serving life and through prayer and spiritual work, particularly through the use of the violet flame.

It is well to remember that if you do meet your twin flame, this will not solve all your problems. In fact, you will likely also meet the karma that separated you in the first place. If you allow karma or human habits or momentums to overwhelm your love, you may find that your problems become greater rather than less when you meet the beloved.

Meeting your twin flame may not solve all of your problems. But all problems may be solved in the crucible of the love of twin flames. It all depends on what you make of the opportunity.

The Inner Relationship
of Twin Flames

I n all likelihood, you and your twin flame meet at inner levels at night while your body sleeps and your soul travels to the temples of light in the heaven-world. Some people have memories of these meetings when they awaken in the morning or dreams that recall pure and blissful moments with the beloved. These soul encounters may take place whether you have conscious recall of them or not.

The reality is that twin flames are always united at inner levels, even if they are separated by outer circumstances. Your Higher Self and the Higher Self of your twin flame are the magnets that will draw you together—in this world, if possible, and certainly in the next. And your inner contact with the beloved can magnify your light and attainment, giving new strength to face all the challenges of life.

So keep on striving to be true to your Higher Self. Ask God to help you balance your karma and perfect your soul in divine love—and offer the same prayer for your twin flame. Your mission, your twin flame and your ultimate reunion in the heart of God await you.

You can accelerate your spiritual progress and your reunion with your twin flame, wherever that beloved one is, if in your prayer and meditation you call to your Higher Self for the inner heart contact with your twin flame. You can give the following prayer at the beginning of your meditation or prayer time or before you retire at night:

In the name of the Christ, I call to the blessed God Presence of our twin flames for the sealing of our hearts as one for the victory of our mission. I invoke the light of the Holy Spirit and the violet flame for the consuming of all negative karma limiting the full expression of our divine identity and the fulfillment of our divine plan. And I claim our victory now!

According to God's holy will, let it be done.[2]

In saying this prayer, even if you live in separate worlds in time and space, you can unite spiritually on higher planes. You can direct light into your own world and the world of your twin flame for the balancing of karma and the fulfillment of your divine destiny.

Soul Mates

When people hear of soul mates, they sometimes think that this is another term to describe the relationship of twin flames. In fact, a soul-mate relationship is different from that of twin flames. A soul mate is just what the words say: a mate of the soul. Soul mates are partners for the journey.

Soul mates may have been together in past lives and developed a strong bond or connection of love. They often come together because they are working on he same type of karma and developing mastery of the same energies.

A soul mate is like the echo of oneself in the matter plane. Soul mates have a complementary calling or mission in life. Their love is often expressed in the work they do together. They join forces for a period of time or even a lifetime or more—for a marriage or business venture, a book or invention, or some other project. Thus, although you have only one twin flame, you may have more than one soul-mate relationship in your many lifetimes. A soul-mate relationship does not necessarily result in marriage; however, if marriage between soul mates is in the cards, such a marriage is often a very loving, harmonious and productive match.

Some of the great love stories of history are of soul mates.

The love of Arthur and Guinevere formed the nucleus of Camelot and the mystery school of the Knights of the Round Table. Mary and Joseph, the parents of Jesus, were soul mates who came together to share the responsibility for nurturing the Christ within their son.

One woman I knew had the experience of meeting both her twin flame and a soul mate in this life. She told me the story of these two relationships and where they led her.

Rachel was in her twenties when she met David. They were attracted to one another and had a brief relationship as their careers intersected, but the relationship did not last. They both moved on, their lives taking them in different directions, but somehow Rachel couldn't entirely forget David.

Some years later, Rachel took up the spiritual path in earnest and she came to understand that David was her twin flame, something she had not known when they were together. She contacted him again and spoke about the inner connection between them, but he didn't seem to understand. He was not interested in spiritual things and no longer felt a connection with her.

Rachel understood that she had a choice. She could try to reestablish the connection with David. It was possible that he would respond to her love and they could be together, but in order to do this she would need to leave the spiritual community that was her home. She would need to set aside her own spiritual path for a time, or at least pursue it with much less intensity. Would she, herself, be able to make it on the path if she made this sacrifice? Would she be able to help raise him up to the point where he would also be interested in pursuing a spiritual path? Or would he pull her back to involvement in worldly things? There were no guarantees.

Rachel chose to continue in her path and to let David pursue his own course in life. Rachel says that it was incredibly hard to make the decision to leave her twin flame and move forward with her life, but she has no regrets. Some people might see this as selfish, but Rachel felt that best hope was for one of them, at least, to pursue the path. She could then provide a spiritual anchor for David at the time when he might also decide to pursue the path. She knew that if she followed him in his current direction in life, they might both go down, caught up in the ways of the world.

Some years later, God provided a soul mate to be a companion on her journey. She met Vincent. They fell in love, and after a romantic and exciting courtship they married. They have carved out a wonderful life together. She has not told Vincent about her twin flame as it is not necessary to burden him with this knowledge.

"Vincent and I are very happy together," she says. "We work at keeping the love that we share in our marriage, and we share one another's burdens in life. We travel together and I support him in his work as he does in mine. It is a great match. He often surprises me with flowers and gifts and he makes me laugh. We complement one another and I could not be happier."

Karmic Partners

The third kind of relationship is the one that arises from karmic ties.

We all have relationships with people with whom we have made karma in past lives—good karma and bad karma. A karmic debt is felt at the soul level. Somehow the soul knows when there are karmic ties that need to be undone, negative energy to balance, the wrong corrected and the hurt healed. We may not know exactly what transpired in a past life (and most often it is not necessary to know), but we sense the need to resolve through love.

Romantic relationships arising from karma may be intense, and there may be a great attraction and even a great love. They may also be very difficult. Sometimes the worse the karma, the more intense the attraction when we first meet. This comes from the soul's inner desire to set that one free from a burden we have caused in the past. We love much because there is much to be forgiven.

The story of Sarah and Jim illustrates these elements in a karmic marriage. Sarah was in her seventies when she told me this story. She had met Jim when they were in their late teens and there was an instant attraction between them. They had an intense affair, married and soon had three children. After a period of time, Sarah realized that although she loved Jim, he did not return her love in the same way. She felt that they were falling out of love.

Life together became increasingly difficult—they disagreed about almost everything. Jim smoked and she did not; Sarah was drawn to a spiritual life and he was not. Gradually they realized that they were very different in many ways. He took other lovers, but nevertheless they persisted in the marriage.

Eventually they developed an arrangement that worked for them. Jim provided for Sarah and did not prevent her from pursuing her spiritual endeavors. She in turn cared for him, the children and the home, cooked, cleaned and took care of many details of daily life so that he could continue in his successful business.

Still, it was very difficult. She knew that this relationship was a means for her to balance karma, but was it really the most important thing she could do in life? Was there a higher calling that she was missing out on? She prayed deeply to know if she should stay or leave.

As she prayed, she was shown that they had been together more than once in past lives. In their most recent embodiment, he had been cruel to her and she in desperation had wounded him and left him to die.

In this life, they had been brought together so that they could balance their karma from that lifetime and many others. This karmic debt could be best resolved in the intensity and love of the relationship of husband and wife. She received the strong impression that she should continue in the marriage until there was a clear indication that the karmic debt had been resolved.

This revelation helped Sarah to endure the situation and

continue in the marriage, to love Jim with an unselfish love. She knew that he was not her twin flame or soul mate, but she wanted them both to be free at the conclusion of their marriage, whenever that might be.

Shortly thereafter, Jim became ill, the end result of a lifetime of poor health habits. She honored her marriage vows, "for better or for worse, in sickness and in health." She lovingly cared for him. He was grateful for her love, and she noticed that there was a softening of his gruff exterior. She, in turn, discovered an inner peace that had previously eluded her.

Romantic relationships arising from karma may be intense, and there may be a great attraction and even a great love. We love much because of our soul's desire to set that one free from a burden we have caused in the past.

Jim soon learned that his illness was terminal. Sarah knew that she would receive the home and all that they had worked for when he passed on, but this in no way motivated her actions and her decision to continue to stay with him. Rather, she learned that the law of karma is exact, and she understood that providing for her financial security was a means for Jim to balance his karma with her.

Their life continued as it was and she prayed deeply for him each day. She was at his side when he peacefully died. After fifty-one years, the marriage was over.

The story did not end there. Several weeks after Jim passed, Sarah was in meditation. She saw him come to her side in his spiritual light-body. He bent down and kissed her on the cheek several times and conveyed his gratitude for her loving care and wisdom.

After death he was able to communicate to her what he had

been unable to see in life. She had understood their relationship at a deeper level than had been possible for him. He was grateful for many reasons and wanted her to know it now. She was pleased beyond words to know that he was fine and that her karmic obligation to him had been fulfilled.

As Sarah reflected on her life, she said to me, "Our marriage was a God-given opportunity to develop compassion and to balance our karma together. As hard and as painful as it was, I would not have changed it for the world. I thank God that I had the sense to stay with him and balance the karma."

Today, Sarah recognizes her decision to stay with Jim might not be the choice that someone else might make in similar circumstances, but she maintains that staying with him was an assignment that she was given by her angels before she took embodiment. All in all, it was the best thing for both of them.

Ultimately the soul knows whether to leave or to endure. Sarah is a strong soul and she was not a doormat in their relationship. Jim was never abusive and she was fully aware of the situation that she faced. For a different person in a different situation, it may be the right thing to leave. If there is any concern about abuse or physical, mental or emotional harm to oneself or one's children, then take the steps that are needed to ensure the safety of yourself and your loved ones.

The unexpected ending to this story is that several years later, Sarah met a soul mate. They married and are now happily making a life together in their seventh decade. "The universe never fails to surprise me," Sarah said. "And I like to be surprised."

A marriage of karma may not have the depth of the relationship between twin flames or soul mates, but such a marriage can also be the means for the expression of a great and transforming love. It can be for a liberation of the soul, as it was in the case of Sarah.

It is not necessarily a tragedy when people have difficult circumstances or karma to work through. It is a tragedy when they do not use the opportunity these challenges provide for love, forgiveness and healing, when they ignore the promptings of the soul and stay when they should leave, or walk away before an assignment is completed.

Resolving the Past

The relationship of Sarah and Jim had all the hallmarks of a karmic marriage, where two individuals are drawn together for the balancing of mutual karma. Karmic relationships are often difficult, but they can lead to great growth for the soul and mastery on the spiritual path. They also provide the opportunity to make good karma through service together and through sponsoring and nurturing children.

Some of these marriages provide the opportunity for the balancing of the karma of severe crimes, such as betrayal, extreme hatred or murder. These karmas may also involve others who were affected in these situations. Sometimes the only way the soul can overcome the record of such hatred is by the intense love and mutual service expressed through the relationship of husband and wife.

However, in many cases it is possible through service and the use of the violet flame to balance mutual karma without the necessity of a marriage relationship. This is often a better way. And even if the karmic law does decree that marriage should take place, spiritual work, including the use of the violet flame, can smooth the way and ease the burdens of karma.

Susie, a medical student on the West Coast, recalls meeting Brad, a trainee radiologist from the East Coast who was working at her hospital. Brad had moved to Susie's town on an impulse two weeks before they met, and as soon as he saw her he recognized her as someone he wanted to have a relationship with.

Brad was tall, good looking and well built. He had a gentle and humorous way about him and all the nurses were trying to catch his eye, but he only had eyes for Susie. She was not attracted to him at all. In fact, she didn't want to have anything to do with him. He kept pursuing her and eventually she relented. She agreed to some dates, thinking that he would soon realize that they were not at all suited and would move on to someone else.

After a couple of dates, she became aware of a past life where they had been together in Scotland. Brad had deserted her and had an affair with her best friend. She had died alone and afraid, giving birth to his child. She hated him then for his betrayal, and she had carried that feeling over into this life. Now she understood that they owed one another a debt of karma.

Back in this life, Susie understood the pain that Brad was feeling. As she prayed about the situation, she desired to no longer hate Brad but to help him to balance their karma together. She even began to like him, even though she knew she would never marry him. She knew it was a karmic tie, and she decided not to have a romantic relationship with him. Instead, she supported him as a friend.

Brad's previous girlfriend had dumped him right before his last attempt at passing his medical boards and he had failed his exams. Susie remained supportive as he readied himself to try again and helped him to study. He passed his boards and became a fully qualified radiologist.

He planned to move to England and wanted her to go with

him. She declined. She told him that they each had other people waiting for them. She also told him that although he might not understand it now, one day he might want to ask for her forgiveness for a past life transgression and she would not be there to ask. She said, "When that day comes, Brad, know that I have already forgiven you."

Susie credits the angels with moving Brad from one side of the country to the other so that they could meet and resolve their karma. She is also grateful that she had the wisdom to not enter a romantic involvement that could have created more karma and been a major detour from her life plan. Both of them are now happily married, living in different countries, scarcely thinking of the other or maintaining contact.

Our souls know why we have come into embodiment. Before we entered into a new body, angel guides explained the karmic situations that needed resolution. The soul has a strong inner desire to right these wrongs, since this is the only way to return to the heavenly home and to the perfect love we seek.

These karmic situations may come to us as romantic involvements, family relationships, business partnerships, friendships, and all the varied interactions of our lives. No matter what the situation, providing love and assistance, service and helpfulness to everyone we meet, combined with liberal use of the violet flame, is an excellent way to balance karma, free ourselves from these burdens and promote our progress on the spiritual path.

The Violet Flame

One key for getting through past karma and fulfilling your mission is the use of the violet flame. The violet flame is a manifestation of the Holy Spirit, a spiritual energy given by God to man for the acceleration of consciousness. It transforms negative energy into positive energy—anger into love, irritation into peace, suspicion into trust, darkness into light.

In his book *The Chela and the Path*, the Eastern adept El Morya explains the origin and nature of the violet flame:

> The violet flame comes forth from the violet ray, that aspect of the white light that is called the seventh ray. It is indeed the seventh-ray aspect of the Holy Spirit. Just as the sunlight passing through a prism is refracted into the rainbow of the seven color rays, so through the consciousness of the Holy Spirit the light of the Christ is refracted for mankind's use in the planes of Matter.
>
> Each of the seven rays is a concentrated, activating force of the light of God having a specific color and frequency. Each ray can also manifest as a flame of the same color and vibration. The application of the flame results in a specific action of the Christ in body and soul, mind and heart.[3]

When you visualize this violet flame and call it forth into your consciousness, it begins to change negative energy patterns accumulated over thousands of lifetimes. You begin to experience feelings of joy, lightness and hope as the negative energy is transmuted. It's as if your consciousness were being purified by a fire that burns the karma of centuries. And that's exactly what is happening with this alchemical fire of God's light and love.

The violet flame can literally dissolve mountains of karma. Kara, who we met on previous pages, used the violet flame to balance and transmute her karma with Robert, the father of her three children. She credits the violet flame for a large degree of

It may be that the only thing keeping you from reunion with your twin flame is the use of the violet flame to clean up some karma.

the peace and equanimity that she now feels after going through the harrowing experience of divorce after a painful relationship.

There are many ways to use the violet flame. You can meditate on the violet flame, seeing yourself standing in violet light, the energy passing through you and dissolving all negativity. You can also visualize the violet flame around another person. If you have a difficult situation with an acquaintance, friend, co-worker or family member, visualize the violet flame around both of you. See it transmuting karma and negative momentums from the past, clearing up misunderstandings, smoothing the rough places and removing all barriers to the best resolution.

Even more effective is to combine these visualizations with the science of mantra. When you invoke the flame physically through the spoken Word,* its action is stronger and comes

---

* *Word* with a capital *W* is used to describe the Logos, the power of God. John's gospel opens with the words "In the beginning was the Word ..." The science of the spoken Word is a means to bring that power into physical manifestation.

into physical manifestation more quickly. Buddhists, Hindus, Greek Orthodox monks, Catholic saints and Jewish mystics have all found a greater access to the Higher Mind and a state of oneness with God through the repetition of mantras, chants, prayers and decrees.

The primary purpose of this science is to put you in contact with your Higher Self. Once you have that contact, you can draw on the power of the God to create positive change for yourself, for your relationships and for the world around you. When the spoken Word is combined with meditation and visualization, the results can be extraordinary.

Here is a simple violet-flame mantra—also known as a decree. It is easy to remember and you can give it any time as a means for dealing with negative energy.

I AM a being of violet fire!
I AM the purity God desires!

This can be given strongly as a fiat or repeated as a chant, visualizing the light of the violet flame around yourself or whatever situation to which you are sending it. Visualize the flame penetrating and dissolving all negativity, leaving yourself and everyone involved manifesting nothing but the purity God desires for that situation.

The "I AM" in this decree is more than a positive statement. It is an affirmation of the God within you. "I AM" is the name that God revealed when he spoke to Moses out of that burning bush. "I AM THAT I AM.... Say unto the children of Israel, I AM hath sent me unto you.... This is my name for ever, and this is my memorial unto all generations."[4] Therefore, when you say, "*I AM* a being of violet fire," you are affirming, "*God in me* is a being of violet fire." You are consciously releasing God's energy anchored in your heart as the violet flame.

Try giving this decree or any of the other violet-flame decrees in this book for ten or fifteen minutes a day. See how it makes a difference in your life, transmuting blocks and accelerating your consciousness. The violet flame can go a long way toward consuming layers of negative energy and karma that stand between you and the one you are supposed to be with in this life.

On the next two pages are two more violet-flame decrees. Give the opening prayer or invocation for each decree and then repeat the verse section three times, nine times or as many times as you wish while you visualize the flame, as spiritual fire, surrounding you and your twin flame or entering into any situation that requires resolution. Conclude with the sealing and acceptance.

I AM the Violet Flame

In the name of my own God Presence, I AM in me, and my Holy Christ Self, Mighty I AM Presence and Holy Christ Self of my twin flame, I call to Saint Germain and all the masters and angels of the violet flame to expand the violet flame within my heart, purify my four lower bodies, transmute all misqualified energy I have ever imposed upon life, blaze mercy's healing ray throughout the earth and all mankind, and answer this my call for me and my twin flame infinitely, presently, and forever.

I AM the violet flame
In action in me now
I AM the violet flame
To light alone I bow
I AM the violet flame
In mighty cosmic power
I AM the light of God
Shining every hour
I AM the violet flame
Blazing like a sun
I AM God's sacred power
Freeing every one

And in full faith I consciously accept this manifest, manifest, manifest! (3x) right here and now with full power, eternally sustained, all-powerfully active, ever expanding and world enfolding until all are wholly ascended in the light and free!

Beloved I AM! Beloved I AM! Beloved I AM!

The Law of Forgiveness

Beloved mighty victorious Presence of God, I AM in me, beloved Holy Christ Self, beloved heavenly Father, in the name and by the power of the Presence of God which I AM and by the magnetic power of the sacred fire vested in me, I call upon the law of forgiveness and the violet transmuting flame for each transgression of thy Law, each departure from the sacred covenants. Restore in me the Christ mind, forgive my wrongs and unjust ways, make me obedient to thy code, let me walk humbly with thee all my days. In the name of the Father, the Mother, the Son and the Holy Spirit, I decree for all whom I have ever wronged and for all who have ever wronged me:

> Violet fire, enfold us! (3x)
> Violet fire, hold us! (3x)
> Violet fire, set us free! (3x)

I AM, I AM, I AM surrounded by
a pillar of violet flame,
I AM, I AM, I AM abounding in
pure love for God's great name,
I AM, I AM, I AM complete
by thy pattern of perfection so fair,
I AM, I AM, I AM God's radiant flame
of love gently falling through the air.

> Fall on us! (3x)
> Blaze through us! (3x)
> Saturate us! (3x)

And in full faith I consciously accept this manifest, manifest, manifest! (3x) right here and now with full power, eternally sustained, all-powerfully active, ever expanding and world enfolding until all are wholly ascended in the light and free!

Beloved I AM! Beloved I AM! Beloved I AM!

2
Love, Light and Energy

The experience of true Love rests upon your free will....

Almighty God ... created you out of his very being and sacred fire—you and your beloved. Take responsibility for your wants and lacks and fill the void with devotion and prayer. Ascend the scale of being until you are ready for the trials and the triumphs of a perfect Love.

CHAMUEL AND CHARITY
ARCHANGELS OF LOVE

Beyond the Physical Body

N ow that we have described the basic types of connections that bring people together, let's look in more detail at the spiritual energies that come into play in relationships through the aura, the chakras, and the finer bodies of man.

In the world today, there is much talk of love, but often this is focused on physical attraction or sensual love. Those who are truly in love know that love goes beyond the boundaries of the physical. Divine lovers are not so concerned with the physical appearance of the beloved, for they see beyond the body. They love the soul and recognize that the body is simply a house for the soul and spirit.

We are all much more than our physical bodies. We are souls sent forth from God to experience life in the material world. We have a physical body through which we can do this. We also have an emotional body (known as the astral body) through which we feel; a mental body through which we think; and an etheric body, or memory body, in which is recorded all of our past, including records of past lives. These four lower bodies are interpenetrating sheaths of consciousness that clothe the soul.

Beyond this, there are even higher levels of consciousness, planes beyond the realms of time and space. These are the three higher bodies of pure spirit. Collectively they are known as the Higher Self.

The relationship between the lower self and the Higher Self is illustrated in the Chart of Your Divine Self, shown on the facing page. The soul clothed in the four lower bodies is the lower figure in the Chart. The Higher Self consists of the middle figure and the upper figure.

At the center of the upper figure is the I AM Presence, the presence of the living God that is individualized for each of us. The I AM Presence is surrounded by spheres of light known as the causal body—spheres within spheres, our treasures stored in heaven, all the good that we are and ever have been.

The middle figure in the Chart is the Holy Christ Self. This is the consciousness of Christ within us—the inner guide, the inner teacher, our chief guardian angel. The Higher Self is a representation of the consciousness of Christ, of Buddha, of the eternal light. When we listen to our Higher Self, we make better decisions and life goes better. When we ignore that prompting, which often comes to us as a still, small voice within, the voice of conscience, then we have problems.

We all have within us a highest ideal of the beloved—the knight, the champion, the lady of the flame. This image is an archetype that represents the Holy Christ Self of our twin flame.

The three higher bodies and the four lower bodies comprise the seven bodies of man. The number seven is a mystical number; it is no accident that there are seven days of the week, seven colors of the rainbow, seven energy centers in the body of man and seven bodies. The spiritual world is mirrored in the material world and in our own physical body.

With this understanding we can see why love is often such an intense experience. We are experiencing love in all four of the lower bodies—in our feeling and thinking world and in our

The Chart of Your Divine Self

memory as well as with the physical senses. And in its most profound expression, love is an interchange at the level of the Higher Self as well.

We are all seeking love, and yet we may not realize that love is also seeking us. Perhaps you feel an absence of love or sense of loss or loneliness. This hollow feeling may not be only the absence of a partner in life, but even more the longing for your beloved counterpart in heaven, your own Higher Self.

All of life is one at levels of pure Spirit, and when you pursue a closer relationship with God and with your Higher Self, you begin to feel that sense of oneness with all life. You begin to draw to yourself more and more of your mission and plan.

You are intended to have a loving relationship with your Higher Self and with God. Once you have this relationship, it affects everything you do and everyone you meet for the better. The difference this can make in your life can be profound. As Mary Baker Eddy has said, "Divine Love always has met and always will meet every human need."[1]

Your Seven Energy Centers

Within our body are seven major energy centers, called *chakras*. These spiritual centers regulate the flow of God's energy throughout our four lower bodies. It is within these centers that we experience the flow of love, of light, of spiritual energy.

The seven major chakras are positioned along the spinal column from the base of the spine to the crown. Each chakra is symbolically depicted as a lotus, each with a different number of petals. The more petals the chakra has, the higher its frequency or vibration.

Chakras are not static points of light but dynamic energy centers that constantly take in, store and send out spiritual light. The flow of this light affects the size and quality of the aura. The correct use and care of these subtle energy centers leads to greater vitality in our physical body as well as the mental, emotional and etheric bodies.

Every day we make choices as to how to use the energy God sends to us through the crystal cord that connects us with our Higher Self. These daily choices—how we love, the words we speak, the thoughts we think and the actions we take—determine the energy we send out into the world that will one day return to us as karma, both bad and good. And just as choices

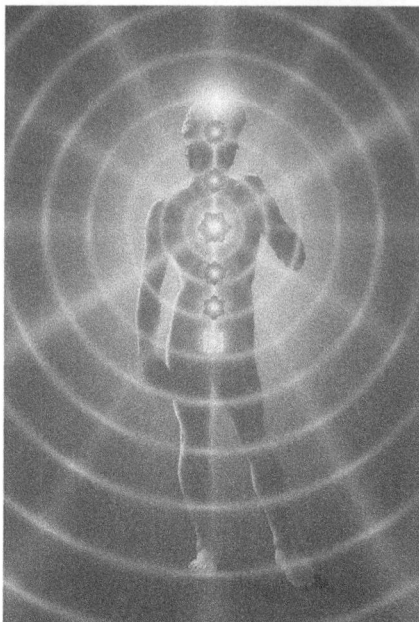

of diet and lifestyle affect the health and vitality of the physical body, how we use the energy of the chakras can greatly influence the flow of spiritual energy in our life.

The chakras are shown in this illustration as radiating centers of light, as they would appear in the purified etheric body. In ascending order along the spine, the seven chakras and their pure colors are: base of the spine (white), seat of the soul (violet), solar plexus (purple and gold), heart (pink), throat (blue), third eye (green), and crown (yellow).

The heart center is the most important energy center in the body. It is the hub of life, physically and spiritually. Just as blood is pumped by the physical heart to the rest of the body, so all of the energy we receive from God passes through our heart chakra before it moves on to nourish the other chakras and systems of our finer bodies.

The heart is also the place where we experience love, both human and divine. We know this intuitively. We speak of winning someone's heart, a tender heart, a heart full of love, a broken heart. Love is symbolized as a heart ♥.

Of course it is not merely the physical heart that is the focus of love. The real center of love is the twelve-petaled chakra in the center of the chest, the spiritual center associated with the physical heart.

If we focus our energies in the heart, we can build a greater magnet of love. Just as we exercise the physical heart, we can also exercise the spiritual heart so that it can give and receive more love. Here is a mantra and meditation to build a greater magnet of love in the heart.

I AM the Light of the Heart

I AM the Light of the Heart
Shining in the darkness of being
And changing all into the golden treasury
Of the Mind of Christ.

I AM projecting my Love
Out into the world
To erase all errors
And to break down all barriers.

I AM the power of infinite Love,
Amplifying itself
Until it is victorious,
World without end!

Light Is the Magnet

We are intended to garner light in the heart and in all of our chakras for our use in fulfilling our divine plan and our mission in life. This light also becomes a magnet that can attract everything we need for the fulfillment of that plan and mission—including the right partner in life. However, at the end of the day, many people have a net loss of light in their auras and spiritual centers. They lose light on a daily basis instead of storing it in their chakras and using it for positive purposes.

There are many ways to lose this light. When we are critical, unloving or inharmonious, the light of the chakras is misused and lost. When we become angry or let loose with a tirade of abuse, we lose light. We may lose light in the throat chakra with unkind or angry words, in the solar-plexus chakra through the misuse of emotional energy, or in the heart through turning love to hatred.

Our lifestyle choices also affect the amount of light we carry. For example, if we smoke tobacco, this not only damages our physical health but also interferes with the functioning of the third-eye chakra and the crown. If we choose to take drugs or alcohol, we not only risk becoming addicted, we also experience a loss of light because these substances can create holes or tears in our auric forcefield and spiritual centers.

Another way to lose light is through relationships that are not healthy for us. Many of us recall a friendship or relationship where we felt used. In the end we realized that the other person was not concerned about us and was simply taking what he or she could—physically, emotionally or spiritually. In simple terms, these kinds of people take light from our aura, if we let them. The more deeply we are involved with them, the more light we may lose.

We can lose light from a misuse of any of the chakras, and that loss of light produces a downward spiral that can culminate in problems of many kinds. We may feel weary, tired or listless, unmotivated, easily discouraged or depressed. When we don't have the light we should, we lose the sense of joy and purpose in life. Ultimately, we have less energy for the activities and projects we really want to do. Losing our light also makes us less attractive to others and gives us the tired and spent look often seen in those who overindulge in negative habits.

Most people understand how this works for the physical body. They realize that if they look after the body with good food and exercise, they will have more vitality and better health. Think how different the world would be if people put as much effort into spiritual health as the health of the physical body—if they were as concerned about keeping their auras as clean as their clothes.

The light of the eye, the light of the chakras, our mental and emotional health—all of these are at least as important as physical health in the long term. Spiritual exercise is the means to bring more light to the aura and all levels of consciousness, including the physical body. And ultimately, it is the light within the aura that is the magnet that draws people together, even more than mere physical appearance.

The following mantra can be used to expand the light of the aura and the chakras. As you say the words, see and feel the actions they describe taking place within you.

I AM Light

I AM Light, glowing Light,
Radiating Light, intensified Light.
God consumes my darkness,
Transmuting it into Light.

This day I AM a focus of the Central Sun.
Flowing through me is a crystal river,
A living fountain of Light
That can never be qualified
By human thought and feeling.
I AM an outpost of the Divine.
Such darkness as has used me is swallowed up
By the mighty river of Light which I AM.

I AM, I AM, I AM Light;
I live, I live, I live in Light.
I AM Light's fullest dimension;
I AM Light's purest intention.
I AM Light, Light, Light
Flooding the world everywhere I move,
Blessing, strengthening, and conveying
The purpose of the kingdom of heaven.

The Base Chakra

One of the most important chakras to understand is the base-of-the-spine chakra. Many people lose a lot of light through this chakra—especially through inordinate sexual activity. All too often they seem driven by their desires and in particular by their sexual impulses. They may be looking for love and a relationship of the heart, but they end up in sexual liaisons and relationships at the level of the base chakra.

Of all of the seven chakras, this is frequently the one we have the most difficulty mastering. It often brings the most grief into our world through painful relationships and a loss of light. But when we understand the purpose of this chakra and we gain some mastery of its energy, there are great rewards.

The sages of the East teach that the there is a primal spiritual life-force known as the *Kundalini* that is sealed within the chakra at the base of the spine. Here we experience the power of creation and the ability to procreate.

The base chakra is the lowest point to which the light descends on the spinal column. It is the location of the white light, or the white fire, which is, spiritually speaking, sacred energy, or sacred fire. In fact, sexual energy is sacred energy. Sexual intercourse is intended to be a sacred union between the energies of man and woman.

The light of the Kundalini is not intended to stay only in the base chakra. It is meant to be raised up the spine, nourishing and activating each chakra along the way, causing the "wheel" of the chakra to spin, the "lotus" to blossom.

This light is intended to amplify and strengthen the positive expression of each chakra in turn. In the base chakra, this light is expressed as purity, discipline, wholeness and the integration of our spiritual and physical beings. In the seat-of-the-soul chakra, this light strengthens and heals the soul and the expression of freedom, mercy, forgiveness, alchemy and intuition.

In the solar plexus, this light strengthens the emotional body and the expression of right desire, peace, brotherhood and selfless service. In the heart chakra, this light is expressed as love, compassion, creativity, charity and generosity.

The throat chakra is the center of power, faith, will, direction and courage. Through the third-eye chakra, this light is expressed as truth, vision, clarity, abundance, science, music and the ability to precipitate from spirit to matter. The crown chakra is the center of wisdom, illumination, self-knowledge and cosmic consciousness.

Every day we receive from our Higher Self an allotment of spiritual energy. This energy enables us to think, feel, speak, act and fulfill our purpose in life. We have free will to decide what to do with this energy that flows to us each day.

We can raise that light in our spiritual centers to support all that we wish to achieve in all levels of consciousness. We can also dissipate that energy in any one of our chakras through unbalanced activities that do not add to our spiritual path and that may even harm ourselves or others.

When we conserve the Kundalini energy that resides at the

base-of-the-spine chakra and raise it to nourish our other centers, it can activate new levels of spiritual awareness within us. If we lose this light, we reduce the amount of energy available to rise through the other chakras, and thus the latent power of those chakras remains untapped. If we do not raise it, we will also find that energy collects at the base chakra and demands an outlet.

The buildup of energy at the base chakra can lead to an inordinate focus on sex and the misuse of sexual energy. Some individuals release this energy through misuse of energy in other chakras, such as outbursts of anger, physical abuse, addictions to drugs, or other destructive activities. Even endless chatter can be a manifestation of sexual energy gone awry.

When we conserve the energy that we receive from the Divine Source, it is available to us for creativity in all of its forms. This light enables us to be more joyous and effective in all we do. It is also available to us to attract the best possible partner in life, the one who is divinely ordained to be our helpmate.

Unfortunately, most people today are not taught how to conserve energy in the spiritual centers or to raise the light to higher chakras. Many are burdened by the energy that gathers in the base-of-the-spine chakra because they do not know how to deal with it.

Later in this book we will examine spiritual techniques that can help us conserve the sacred fire that is the spiritual energy of the base chakra and to raise it to the higher centers.

Sex Is Not a Sin

One of the burdens we face living in the West is the concept that sex and sexual activity are sinful in themselves and that they have something to do with "original sin."

This isn't something that is found in the Bible. In fact, the "original sin" of Adam and Eve (whose story portrays in allegory the fall of man) was disobedience to the laws that God had set for their spiritual path in the Mystery School that was known as the Garden of Eden.

Having disobeyed and left off from their path of initiation, they knew that they were "naked" because they had lost the original light of the aura that was the garment of the soul. Since they could no longer remain in their paradise in the heaven world, the Bible recounts that God made for them "coats of skins"—in actuality, the physical, mental and emotional bodies that would serve as the vehicles for the soul in lower realms.

Early Christian theologians, not understanding the nature of the allegory and its lessons, interpreted the story of Adam and Eve in a very literal way. In the face of all evidence to the contrary, they decided that Adam and Eve were the first man and woman on earth and that they lived around 4,000 B.C. They also concluded that the original sin of Adam and Eve was sex. We have been living with this burden about sex ever since.

Rightly understood, sex is not sinful. It is simply energy in motion. The word *sex* can be thought of as a code for *sacred energy exchange (s-e-x)*. The act of sexual intercourse is an exchange of sacred energy. It is holy and sacred if those who participate in it so consecrate it and revere it.

However, this sacred energy can also be misused, and when it is misused we do make karma. We can also create an imbalance in our base chakra if we have an inordinate focus on sexual activity or an inordinate guilt or fear of sexuality. It is for this reason that all spiritual traditions include guidelines for the right use of sexual energy. Most also teach that sex, in balance and in the right context, is healthy and even sacred when it is held within a circle of commitment and the vows of marriage.

Sacred sexuality can be an intimate experience with God and with the divine energy residing within us and within our partner if the union is sanctified. For the very reason of the sacredness of the energy of love, it is important to treat our relationships as sacred. This is also the reason that people stand before a representative of God—whether minister, priest or rabbi—for the consecration of their marriage vows.

The Divine Polarity within Us

Many of the world's religions teach us of the feminine or intuitive aspect of ourselves and of God as Mother. The Jewish tradition speaks of the Shekhinah, Hinduism refers to Shakti, Taoism speaks of yang and yin, masculine and feminine principles in all creation. Even Catholicism has a representation of Mother in the female saints, most especially in the person of Mary.

In a larger sense, the physical universe represents the feminine or Mother principle of God, even as the spiritual universe represents the masculine or Father principle. Matter becomes the instrument of Spirit, allowing the unmanifest to become the manifest as the world of form.

The many feminine deities and saints of East and West are personifications of the feminine aspect of God that teach us by example how man and woman can realize their own feminine potential. For both man and woman have a feminine portion of being, the side that develops and maintains relationships, that nurtures, supports, comforts and heals.

The place where God as Mother resides within us is the base-of-the-spine chakra. The energy of the base chakra is referred to as the Mother light. It is the most feminine aspect of being for both man and woman. The corresponding light of

God as Father is anchored in the crown chakra at the top of the head.

In our modern world, the light of Mother is often lost before it can rise when this light is directed into inordinate sexual activity (even early in the teenage years or younger). The light of the Father is lost through the use of alcohol, drugs and tobacco, which damage not only the physical brain but also the spiritual chakras at the crown and third eye.

We are all intended to have a relationship with the divine feminine within us, even as we also have a relationship with the divine masculine. Our outer relationships are intended to support and develop these inner qualities. A woman in his life can help a man to bring out his inner feminine nature—his intuition, empathy and capacity to be gentle and nurturing. In a similar way, a man can help a woman manifest her inner masculine side—her strength, courage and capacity to take thoughtful, decisive action.

When we maintain a vital and balanced flow of energy through the base chakra, we are able to express the qualities of the divine feminine. We are able to care for others and become more sensitive to their needs.

At the level of the base chakra, we can examine our relationship with the feminine aspect of ourselves and with our soul. We might ask ourselves the following questions, whether we are in a female or male body in this life:

Do I honor and respect women?

Am I able to express my intuitive, nurturing side?

Do I take time to nurture myself?

The answers to these questions have a lot to do with our self-mastery of the light of the Divine Mother within the base-of-the-spine chakra. They also have important implications for how we use the life-force and how we express our sexuality.

We might also ask ourselves the following questions, which have to do with our relationship with the energies of Father:

Do I honor and respect men?

Am I able to express my own strength and take decisive action when it is needed?

Do I have the courage to explore new things—even new dimensions of self—and venture outside my comfort zone?

As we have an understanding of yin and yang, of the Divine Father and the Divine Mother within us, we also gain insight into our relationships. As we honor these aspects of our own inner self, we can honor and respect them in others. Both are essential to our growth and wholeness, internally and in our relationships.

The age of Aquarius is the age of the Divine Mother, so as we enter this new cycle, it is especially a time for both man and woman to develop their relationship with the divine feminine. Unless both man and woman are able to express their intuitive side and honor and respect the qualities of the divine feminine, it is unlikely a relationship will support the individuals' spiritual growth in the long term.

The Goal of Life

Mastery of the base-of-the-spine chakra and the light contained there enables us to live a full life, to reach our goals and achieve our highest dreams. It also helps us to attract the partner we are meant to be with for our life's mission.

Yet there is an even higher purpose. When this light and energy are mastered, they become the means for the reunion with the Higher Self. This reunion is the mystical union with God spoken of by saints and mystics.

The sacred light of the Divine Mother sealed in the base-of-the-spine chakra is the energy the soul requires to weave the garment that the soul must have in order to enter into this divine union. This garment is also known in esoteric lore as the *deathless solar body* and the reunion is known as the ascension.

Jesus is an example of one who reunited with the light of God. He demonstrated the ritual of the ascension on Bethany's Hill. However, he is not the only one to have ascended. The Bible records that Elijah was taken up to heaven in "a chariot of fire" and that Enoch, the seventh from Adam, "walked with God: and he was not, for God took him."[2] In heaven there are many others who have also reunited with God. Gautama Buddha, Thérèse of Lisieux, Krishna, Mary the Mother of Jesus,

Saint Germain, Saint Francis, El Morya and countless others, known and unknown, are among those described in the Book of Revelation as "a great multitude ... clothed with white robes."[3]

Many of them were at one time people who lived on earth as we do, and we are intended to follow in their footsteps. They are called ascended masters because they have chosen to master the light and raise it up through the chakras until their whole body, mind and soul became one with God's light. They ascended to "heaven," to the planes of Spirit, to become one with that light.

The ascension is really an acceleration of consciousness— an acceleration of vibration and frequency. It is the process whereby the soul (the feminine aspect of our being), having balanced her karma and fulfilled her divine plan, merges first with the Christ consciousness and then with the living Presence of the I AM THAT I AM (the Spirit, or masculine, aspect of our being).

The joy of the final reunion of the soul with God far transcends anything we can experience on earth. It does include the reunion with one's twin flame.

Once ascended, the soul becomes the Incorruptible One, a permanent atom in the body of God, never to go out again in the rounds of rebirth.

Symbolically and spiritually, the ascension is like a marriage. In fact, it is known as the *alchemical marriage*, and the garment the soul must weave to prepare for this reunion was described by Jesus in parable as the "wedding garment."[4] Through this ritual the soul is reunited with God.

Whatever our outer path in life, the ascension is the ultimate goal of our soul's evolution on earth. And beyond the benefits of happiness and fulfillment, the greatest reason to conserve the sacred fire in all of our spiritual centers is that we need this light and energy to weave the wedding garment, to be ready for the reunion with God at the conclusion of this life.

Those who have achieved this goal tell us that the joy of that final reunion far transcends anything we can experience on earth. It does include the reunion with the twin flame.

It is one thing to know the love and joy of meeting your twin flame here on earth and another entirely to be one with your twin flame in realms of pure Spirit.

The Pull of the Lesser Self

I f the path of light is so clear and simple, if the rewards are so great, why aren't more people walking it? Wouldn't everyone want to experience the bliss of that divine reunion?

The problem is that we have forgotten that this is the goal. Over many lifetimes we have lived in the world and followed its ways. We have allowed ourselves to become angry, to be selfish, to misuse our light. We have indulged in temporary pleasures. We have developed habits, momentums and even addictions. The energy we have fed into these negative patterns has taken on a life and consciousness of its own, which is known in esoteric tradition as the dweller-on-the-threshold.

This lesser self is a part of ourselves that we seldom realize is acting because it usually resides just below the threshold of conscious awareness. We see telltale signs of its presence when we are angry, irritable or out of sorts. It is the lesser self that gets depressed and goads us to say unkind words and perform thoughtless acts, leaving us to wonder how we could have been so cruel.

We all have a Higher Self and a lesser self. And each hour and each day we have the opportunity to choose between these two—light or darkness, wisdom or ignorance, love or hatred, light or anti-light, our divine nature or the lesser self. This is the point where the struggle between good and evil really takes place.

I remember a person who knew about the struggle with the lesser self only too well. He regularly got to the point of being out of control with anger. Too often he found himself erupting at a coworker or just storming out of the room rather than continue a conversation. When he put his fist through a door, he knew he needed help and he started attending anger management classes.

Sometimes the lesser self manifests in more subtle ways. Another person did not like the way she tended to be critical of others and slipped in subtle digs at her friends. She worked hard to bite her tongue and suppress those unkind comments.

> *Although the lesser self can seem very real at times, it is not real in the ultimate sense. It's like a mirage—what they call in the East* maya, *or illusion. Nevertheless, we must learn to deal with the lesser self and its momentums.*

Although it can seem very real at times, the lesser self is not real in the ultimate sense. It's like a mirage—what they call in the East *maya*, or illusion. Yet we must deal with the lesser self and its momentums as long as we live in this realm of time and space.

A life that is centered on the lower self and its desires stops all progress in the evolution of the soul. Sometimes people stagnate like this for many centuries, scarcely giving any thought to God or their own inner reality. This is one reason why it is important for children and youth to have opportunities for spiritual devotions and to give to others in selfless service. Patterns established in those early years often set the sail for an entire embodiment.

Wanting to Be Loved

We all need opportunities to extend our love to others—whether it is helping family members, feeding the homeless, working as a volunteer or in a profession that serves others. As we help others with selfless love, we draw closer to our Higher Self. We feel a greater joy within our heart and a sense of purpose and meaning to life.

We can outwit that lesser self by attuning with our Higher Self and following its direction. And we can remind ourselves that when we finally have our victory, when our soul unites with the Higher Self and returns to heaven, nevermore to go out, then the lesser self will have no place there—it will be gone.

Karmic Cycles

One of the laws of the universe is that energy is neither created nor destroyed. It simply moves and flows and changes from one form to another.

We are continually receiving the energy that descends from our Higher Self over the crystal cord and sending it out into the world. What happens to this energy?

When it returns to us, the energy that we have qualified with light adds to the spheres of our causal body. The energy we have qualified with darkness cannot rise to those spheres. Instead, it accumulates as an energy field that surrounds us in the planes of matter.

This forcefield is called the *electronic belt*. It contains the energies of negative karma that require balancing before the soul can reunite with the I AM Presence. It surrounds the lower portion of each of us and contains the entire record of the negative aspect of the soul's evolution on earth. In form it is like the lower half of an egg positioned from the navel (or the solar plexus) to beneath the feet.

Most of us do not have an outer memory of the soul's experiences in previous lives, for these are hidden below the surface of conscious awareness. However, we become aware of the energies locked up in these experiences when they cycle into our lives for resolution.

The situations we encounter on the streets of life each day are, in reality, the unwinding of the cycles of karma. Both positive and negative forces come full circle for reckoning. When cycles of light return, we can make the most of them, multiply the light and add another increment to our causal body. When cycles of darkness return, this is also an opportunity. We can free this energy from patterns of negativity and requalify it with light.

When past hatreds and animosities and the records of violent interchange surface while we are interacting with another person, we may find ourselves seized with jealousy, anger, resentment, anxiety or any of a multitude of negative reactions. Such experiences are an alert that pockets of energy are surfacing from the subconscious or unconscious, from the electronic belt. When we are aware of this, we can learn to govern those energies that are the records of past mistakes. We have the opportunity to restore balance within ourselves and with others. In the process, we learn the art of self-mastery.

Accidents, injuries, sudden illness, a turn of events in business, in the household or in a marriage may also denote the descent of karma that is released through the cycling of energy from the electronic belt. When we observe this we can know that this is a time to pray, meditate on God and to use the violet flame to transmute these karmic records.

The Chemistry of Attraction

Have you ever met someone and the attraction was instant and magnetic, as if you were being pulled out to sea in an undertow? It can be exciting and disturbing all at the same time. What causes that magnetism or attraction?

As we mentioned earlier, intense attraction can be the result of karma. Karma has a magnetic pull because it is energy that desires to be balanced. God as energy is imprisoned in imperfect patterns, and that energy desires to be free.

The magnetism of negative karma may be felt even as intense love—and sometimes it is only through intense love that intense karma can be balanced. An attraction of karma may lead to falling in love, and the love may last for a shorter or longer period of time. It may last until the karma is balanced, or there may come a period when "the honeymoon is over" and it becomes difficult to hold onto love in the midst of karma.

Individuals may also be attracted not primarily through karma but because they have similar electronic-belt substance, and this forms a polarity at the level of the lower chakras. Such an attraction is often felt as energy in those chakras. Sometimes everyone else in the room is also aware of this magnetism as an "electricity" or sexual tension.

If such an attraction results in sexual intercourse, there will be an exchange of energies in the electronic belt. The energy may spark and discharge, and it may be very intense even as it is fleeting. The electricity will be dissipated, but there is no net gain for the individuals—rather, there is a loss of energy. And there is no exchange of energy at levels of higher consciousness.

But not all attractions are due to negative karma or substance in the electronic belt. There are ties of light and of good karma, and there is the polarity of patterns in the I AM Presence and causal body.

Sometimes there is a feeling or a sense of kinship that comes through a common goal or shared interests. This may also arise from positive karma or momentums of service together in the past. This feeling may progress to a deeper form of friendship or even mutual love. This can happen in twin flame, soul mate or karmic relationships.

There is also what we might think of as the traditional "love at first sight," the immediate soul recognition of a soul mate or twin flame.

One of the challenges of relationships is to discern the nature of attractions and feelings, to follow those that have their origins in a higher source and to be able to resolve and set aside those which would not be productive for the evolution of the soul.

Meeting Your Twin Flame

Valerie and Manuel were both in their fifties when they met for the first time. They saw one another across a room and each recognized the other right away. When they met, they said it was like "coming home." They were twin flames coming together after long lifetimes of separation.

People often imagine that meeting one's twin flame would always be an instant falling in love, as it was for Valerie and Manuel—the stuff of love stories and fairy tales, of seeing a stranger "across a crowded room" and knowing immediately that this is the one.

This may or may not be the case. You can't tell exactly what will happen on the first meeting of twin flames.

There may be an instant recognition, but it is also true that twin flames may or may not recognize each other when they first meet. They may have karma from lifetimes of separation and being apart—and karma blinds. It may not be until the karma is balanced that the couple will recognize one another.

Twin flames may not even like each other when they first meet. Think of Elizabeth Bennet and Mr. Darcy in Jane Austen's *Pride and Prejudice*—two souls who were meant to be together but had an instant aversion for each other. It was not until they could transcend their outer personalities and overcome their prides and prejudices that they could be together.

There have been many instances of twin flames disliking each other when they first met, and the dislike sometimes lasted until they worked through a certain amount of karma and came to recognize the depth of the relationship and the love they shared at inner levels. This was the case with Walter and Eleanor, who we saw earlier in this book.

Sometimes twin flames have such intense karma that they cannot be with each other—the karmic energies are so volatile that love turns to hatred. This is a tragic situation, one which surely brings a tear to the eye of God. There is no relationship more painful to the universe than discord between twin flames.

The lesson of all this is that the recognition of the twin flame often has little to do with falling in love in the usual sense of the word. It is the recognition of an inner soul pattern, the understanding of divine purpose—that here is the other half of the divine Whole. Twin flames may fall in love and later come to understand that nature of the inner relationship, or it may be that falling in love comes some time after the recognition of a destiny together.

Unfortunately, on many occasions people are attracted to a member of the opposite sex primarily by the pull of karma or patterns in the electronic belt. This is often the case when people have not sought a connection with their higher self and have become more attuned to the outer mind, the emotions and the physical senses.

If we seek to walk the spiritual path, sometimes it is necessary to work our way through karmic relationships. But ultimately, we might hope for a relationship based on a higher reality. Making outer plans may not be of much assistance here—there are no five easy steps to find your twin flame. The Higher Self is the only reliable guide. If we can still the mind and emotions sufficiently to listen for the "still, small voice" within, we can receive the inspiration of a higher source. This is usually not a vision of the whole path ahead, but only the next step that leads towards the goal.

Ideally, we should be attracted to our partner by an awareness of a shared destiny. We would hope to recognize the Beloved by the light of the aura and the light in the eyes. When the chakras are cleansed, the aura is purified and the light is raised in the body temple, this is possible.

This does not mean that there is not in such a relationship all of the beauty, joy and bliss of falling in love in every sense of the word. It also does not mean that there is not true and loving sexual attraction between partners. These experiences may all be part of the package. However, the recognition of the relationship between twin flames occurs at a higher level, and the expression of love on other levels grows out of this inner relationship and commitment.

3
Commitment
and Marriage

Whether the union of twin flames, soul mates, or karmic partners, the marriage of man and woman is meant to be mystical, a commemoration of the soul's reunion with the beloved I AM Presence through the Christ, the blessed Mediator.

ELIZABETH CLARE PROPHET

The Marriage Vow

Our love relationships on earth are intended to reflect the marriage of the soul to God. Your divine marriage is also the union of you and your twin flame. This is the true marriage made in heaven.

God has blessed the human institution of marriage as a commemoration of this divine union and as an opportunity for two individuals to develop wholeness. It is precisely because we are not whole that we come together to find wholeness, and the two become one. We may not have the opportunity to meet and marry our twin flame in this life, but this does not alter the spiritual significance of marriage, which is always a commemoration of the union with one's twin flame and the mystical union of the soul with Christ.

The wedding ceremony confers a blessing on the couple which is a reinforcement of their path. But this is only a beginning. And when the vow is taken "for better, for worse, for richer, for poorer, in sickness and in health," this means that we vow to share one another's karma.

The unwillingness to bear one another's burden is often the subconscious reason why people prefer to live together rather than to marry. They say marriage ruins everything, because they know that when they marry they will notice a change in the energy that they bear. In marriage, each side of the party is now bearing the other person's karma and burden. That is the agreement: "I will bear your karma; you will bear mine."

This is why it says in Bible to not be "unequally yoked."[1] Everyone has a different sized sack of karma, and it's really not fair if one partner in the marriage has a bigger sack of karma than the other. It may lead to resentment as the one with less karma ends up carrying the load for the other.

As our karmic cycles unfold, we may have sickness or hardship along the way. Everyone faces this in life at some time. But we realize this is what we have agreed to share. When we take the vow of marriage, it is like placing a stick between our shoulders and we both put our sacks of karma on the stick. There is twice as much karma, but now we have four hands to carry it. And generally when we're walking the path with someone else, we don't get our karma at the same time. So when he has an accident in the car, she makes the appointment for it to be repaired. He takes the car in, she picks it up. We get through it together.

Even as we experience the beauties and the joys of marriage, we also share the unwinding of karma as we travel the road of life together. And we can remember that when something happens, instead of looking at it as "She did it," or "He did it," we can look at it as if it is just part of our own karma, because we are now one and we are now sharing that karma. Even this can be shared in bliss if we have a higher perspective.

As Jesus said, "Sufficient unto the day is the evil thereof"[2] —sufficient unto the day is the karma of that day. Each morning at dawn there is the release of karma, of energy we have to deal with. If we transmute it through service and the use of the violet flame, we can live in the momentum of light that is also released to us each day.

Living Together

Many people today choose to simply live together rather than getting married. Mrs. Prophet offers these insights on what this means from a spiritual perspective:

Marriage requires a commitment. When couples choose to live together without the blessing of marriage, there is actually no commitment except what they say to one another. When you live with someone, any day of the week you or they can walk away from that relationship. Until you pronounce your vows at the altar of marriage, there is not the vow to bear one another's burdens, the burden of karma.

When you are in a relationship where there isn't a marriage, there is an interchange of energy, but there is not necessarily the commitment to bear one another's karma. A love that is really profound and total in a relationship says, "I love you so much that I want to help bear your karma. And I want to bear the burden of your mission."

We go to the altar to be married because we need the intercession of God and his angels and the Holy Spirit in that marriage to help us through the trials and tests that come as we share a burden of karma as well as a burden of service. When we invoke the light of God into the relationship, then that burden can also be one of light—as Jesus meant when he said, "My burden is light."[3]

If you have been married in a civil ceremony, you may wish to reconsecrate your vows before the altar of God. It doesn't matter what church the ceremony takes place in or who is the minister, the rabbi or the priest. When you come in sincerity before God, he will use that instrument and you and your marriage will be blessed. Without this blessing you simply do not have the same spiritual benefit and protection for your relationship.

Sometimes people don't marry because one or the other is thinking, "Well, what if one of these days I want to just get out of here and go somewhere else?" It is the desire to have your freedom but also to have the constancy of a partner. In a certain sense it is a cop-out, because you don't have to take the spiritual responsibilities of a real marriage but you can take its conveniences. In a soul sense, you are cheating yourself.[4]

These kinds of relationships may meet human needs for love and intimacy for a time, but this will be in a limited way, since each one is only prepared to give in a limited way. And we can only receive from a relationship what we are prepared to give to it.

When we are in any relationship, we are investing a certain amount of our energy and we are allowing another to be in a position of polarity with us for the exchange of energy. We want to be sure we're using that energy wisely. This goes for all kinds of relationships and partnerships. Sometimes people enter into a relationship that they know isn't really what they are looking for in the long term. They know they don't want to spend the rest of their life with this person, but the relationship feels good for now. It meets a need until something better should come along.

One down side of this approach is that a relationship like this may well stand in the way of that "something better" ever appearing.

What would happen if you bumped into your twin flame, your soul mate, the one you were meant to be with, but you were already in a relationship? Would you recognize this as the person you were meant to be with? Or would the emotional and physical attraction of the current relationship overwhelm the "still, small voice" telling you that this is the One?

And what about the person you were with? Would you just walk away? What about the pain you would cause them by ending the relationship?

You also have to ask whether that twin flame would recognize you. If you were already in a relationship, he or she might think you were already committed and move on.

It would be a tragedy, but it is an avoidable one if you realize what is happening. By settling for a relationship that you know is not what you are ultimately looking for, you are marking time. You haven't created the space in your life that only your twin flame, your soul mate or your destined partner can really fill. You haven't amplified the magnet of light within to attract that one, since you have used that light to sustain a lesser relationship.

And what if the person you are with is the one destined for you, but you are unwilling to make a greater commitment? A master of the violet flame comments:

> Those who are the adherents of the inner vow have access to a beauty and a joy, a blessedness and a bliss of union that is not shared by those who, in their desire to be free, have greater bondage. Those who make their vow to God have greater light to share....
>
> Where there is a limited giving, there is a limited release. For how can God vow to give himself when individuals cannot vow to give themselves to him or to each other?[5]

The Path of Celibacy

Not everyone is called to the path of marriage in this life. For those who have chosen a path of celibacy, there is a long tradition of coming apart and being separate from society. For centuries holy orders have been places for people to pursue this path. They live with those who have made similar vows, and they live beyond the temptation of the world.

Padre Pio, Thérèse of Lisieux, Francis and Clare, Catherine of Siena, yogis and monks of the East—there are many who have demonstrated a path of devotion and spiritual practice of which celibacy was a part. Their marriage was to God and they experienced the joys of divine love in that purely spiritual union.

In today's world it is perhaps not such an easy thing to come apart and be separate. There are those who are called to the monastic life, but most of us are called by our karma and our life plan to live in the world, and we cannot simply take ourselves off to a monastery and avoid the responsibilities of karma and dharma. Although it may be harder to be celibate in the ordinary bustle of everyday life, many are called to this life and achieve it successfully, even in a worldly setting.

As the light is raised up in this age of Aquarius, we may find the establishment again of such holy orders as existed in ancient times, where those on the celibate path as well as those who are married embrace a holy order and fulfill its sacred purpose. And as they serve to raise the light on earth, they may at the same time take their place in world affairs.

Even those who are not called to a life-long path of celibacy will have periods of celibacy in their lives. This may be in the teenage years, before marriage, during periods of illness or separation in marriage, or after the death or loss of a spouse. So a certain mastery of the sacred fire and the energies of the base chakra is something we are all called to.

In the East, the ancient Vedas speak of four phases of life. In childhood and adolescence one lives as a *brahmacharya*—a period of celibacy as a student. The second stage, *garhasthya*, is that of the married householder with worldly responsibilities, including the raising of children. The third stage, *vanaprastha*, is retirement and meditation, living the life of a hermit or forest-dweller. The final stage, *sannyasa*, is that of renunciation. At the end of life, one lets go of all worldly desires—a wanderer freely pursuing knowledge of Brahman.

It is not uncommon for people to find that these archetypal stages unfold naturally in their lives. Angela was happily married for thirty years until Frank died and she became a widow. Although she has had many offers of marriage she is not even interested in dating anyone. She feels that she has entered another phase of her life and she is happy that she is free to do what she wants to do. Although she misses Frank and the love that they shared, she knows that he is in a better place.

She does not miss the sexual intimacy she once knew, as she has a happy life, serving others, taking care of children as a nanny and being very active physically and in her church. Angela says, "I have found a new way that is right for me and I have no regrets. I believe that this is the path that God would have me follow now, and I am content."

Marriage is not for everyone. Nor is it intended to be. Some are called to the path of celibacy, the path of the adepts, and they are totally content being celibate. They do not have a problem with the sacred fire. Sometimes these are the ones who know at a soul level that they need to follow a celibate path in order to make their ascension.

Simon longed to be married and tended to be drawn to any woman who showed any interest in him. His spiritual teacher talked to him about this one day because she knew he was burdened about not having a partner. Her words were very direct: "Simon, you have had enough sex in all of your lifetimes to last you. If you feel the energies drawing you to someone, I want you to run! and I mean run! the other way—as fast as you can."

Simon realized that his desire to find a mate was not so much the desire of his soul in this life as it was a familiar pattern he had carried over from the past. He took a step back to look at his life and what he really wanted. He took that advice seriously and put his attention on God and his energy into perfecting his talents in service.

If you have squandered much of your light already in this embodiment, if you have had problems with drugs, promiscuity and other means of loss of light from the aura, if this has gone on for many embodiments, then celibacy might be a mandate if you want to attain your ascension in this embodiment. This one factor alone might make the difference in your ascending or not. It is a matter to contemplate in your heart and in your soul.

Whether we choose to be married or celibate, both paths need to be respected and honored, and we need both paths for the spiritual evolution of the planet.

A Problem of Flow

The problem in mastering the sacred fire of the base-of-the-spine chakra is not a problem of sex. It is a problem of flow.

When we speak of flow, we are referring to the flow of light and energy in the body and especially in the chakras. Due to the impressions of the media, through peer pressure, through a focus on sex, many people find an inordinate amount of their energy becomes centered in the base chakra. Rather than accumulating in the lower chakras, this energy should be free to rise in a balanced expression through all of the chakras. When people do not know how to raise this energy, the excess in the lower chakras can become difficult to deal with.

Unfortunately, many people are caught between two worlds. They are not married, but they are not really walking the celibate path. They are somewhere in between and doing neither well. They find that they don't know how to deal with the energies of the base chakra. They end up losing or misusing their light instead of raising it up and finding wholeness within.

If they are intended to be married, they may not have the magnet of their life-force to attract the person who can only be drawn by the light of Christ within. They may find themselves getting older, wanting to be married and worrying about not being married. Yet by not keeping their light, they compound the problem and end up going around in circles.

If you really want to be married, both in the human sense and the divine, you must have an offering of light for the bridegroom or for the bride, who is the consciousness of the Christ in the person who may be waiting for you to arrive at the point of your personal purity.

Of course, it does take effort to master the energies of the base chakra. You may be thinking, "I want to do it, but I can't," or "I don't know how." In fact, we can overcome anything we sincerely want to overcome, but it takes effort and striving, as well as good strategies. And we may have to be willing to wrestle.

We have to get past the sense of unworthiness and even the feeling that we can never overcome this problem or be acceptable to God. This is simply not true. We do not have to accept guilt and shame, and we can overcome.

If raising the light is the life you wish to pursue, don't be burdened or feel guilty if things do not go perfectly at first. Remember that you are a work in progress. Do the best you can and keep striving, even if you do not always get it all right. Ask an understanding friend to pray for you to have the strength to fulfill what you want to achieve. And don't be afraid to ask the angels and the masters to help you.

Prayer and appealing to God and your Higher Self can help very much in the resolution of this situation. You may need to get down on your knees and say to God, "This seems too hard for me. Help me to do better."

Angels came to Jesus in his hour of trial as soon as he made the commitment to follow his calling. They will come to comfort and strengthen you, too, if you make your determination to follow a higher way with sincere effort and striving. Later chapters will offer some spiritual tools and practical techniques to help you.

Finding the Right Path

Marriage, celibacy and the uses and misuses of sexual energy have been misunderstood throughout the ages. This misunderstanding has been the cause of much human misery—often, sadly, in the name of God and religion. Even in our supposedly enlightened age, the meaning of the light of the Divine Mother in relationships is often misunderstood, and yet the problem is as old as time itself.

The Mother light, the sacred fire, the light of the base-of-the-spine chakra, is the same light that was raised up as the foundation of golden ages on the ancient continents of Atlantis and Lemuria. It was the misuse of that light that helped to bring about the downfall of those civilizations. As we enter into a new age, it is the time of the rising once again of that Mother light. And as this light rises, the records and momentums of its misuses are rising again for resolution within us all.

According to Jesus' teachings to us today, it is not necessary for you to be celibate or single or unmarried in order to attain the alchemical marriage (the ascension). In other words, you may be celibate and make your ascension, or you may be married and ascend. Each one needs to find the correct path, the one that is the right one for them.

Celibacy may be very easy for some who have had lifetimes in the Church or in the monasteries of East and West. For others, this may be more difficult to master. You may be comforted to know that the Buddha has said that the test of celibacy and the mastery of the sacred fire was the most difficult initiation that he faced.

We need to look at ourselves in a realistic and practical way. The celibate life is not for everyone, just as married life is not for all. If you have a need to be married, there is no shame or guilt in coming to this conclusion. For many people, marriage is an important part of their divine plan. Jesus himself gave his blessing to the institution of marriage when he performed his first miracle at the marriage feast at Cana.

The path of celibacy and the path of marriage are both legitimate in the eyes of God, and both can be lived in holiness. What has caused many difficulties is the refusal to allow marriage for those who have not had that mastery and that calling—for example, in the Catholic Church, where those who have a calling to the priesthood are required to take a vow of celibacy.

Where did this requirement even come from? The ancient prophets were married, the priests and rabbis of Jesus' time were married (and rabbis are married to this day). The original Vicar of Christ, Peter, was married, and the Apostle Paul says that bishops should be married and have children.[6] Despite all this, church councils hundreds of years after Jesus' time decreed that priests should be celibate.[7]

We see the tragedy of this decision in the scandals that have come out of the Catholic Church in recent years. When there is a lack of understanding of the spiritual principles and methods for raising the light in the chakras, the problem of trying to maintain celibacy can lead to a preoccupation with the base chakra and sexual energy that can be far more of a burden for the soul than the responsibilities of married life.

Celibacy has been considered to be a superior path for those who are able to walk it. This may indeed be a blessing. But if one is called to marriage, this may also be a blessing. In fact, the wholeness found in the balance of man and woman can be a protection to the path of spirituality when couples serve together in holy matrimony.

This is one reason we have marriage upon this earth. We are not yet perfected or whole, and when we serve together, we can help one another. When you are lawfully married, you can dedicate your household to God. You can bring forth children and care for them while pursuing your own self-mastery. Marriage itself exalts and transforms the use of the sacred fire.

Of course, the path of marriage does not exempt us from striving to control the energies of the base chakra and seeking to overcome inordinate sexual desire. There will be times when a couple may not be together and will need to maintain their purity apart from one another. They may also, by mutual agreement, enter into periods of celibacy for periods of devotion, fasting and prayer. We should not seek marriage as a way out, and yet God has provided a way out. All of this is a part of Life's great plan.

Prior to marriage, or if people are not intending to marry, they also have normal sexual needs they must learn to deal with. Many therapists teach that masturbation is a normal part of sexual expression and a healthy outlet for these sexual energies. They see it as a way to deal with sexual tension (which is actually the result of energy accumulating in the base chakra).

However, this can actually perpetuate the underlying problem, which has to do with flow and the mastery of energy. Instead of learning to raise the energy to the upper chakras, this practice is a way of releasing it in the lower chakras. It tends to reinforce the accumulation of energy in those chakras and deprives the upper chakras of the light and energy they need for their best and highest use.

With this understanding, masturbation does not assist in the development of the soul nor does it assist the soul in the upward path. Rather than raising the energy of the Kundalini to God-inspired and creative expression, this practice focuses the attention on sexual desire. It is a means whereby the spiritual light of the body is lost and dissipated.

The deathless solar body required for the ascension is woven day by day from the energy of the base-of-the-spine chakra. It is by raising up the energies of the Mother that you attain your ascension. Therefore, if that energy is constantly released, constantly given away, there is the draining of the light that is meant for the weaving of the soul's wedding garment.

Rather than stimulating and physically releasing the energies of the lower chakras, which wastes the precious energy of the life-force, the ultimate resolution of sexual energy is in the raising of that sacred fire so that it can find positive expression through the higher chakras. Devotion to God through meditation, invocation and decrees for the raising of the Kundalini fire not only resolves the energy physically, but also quickens the spiritual consciousness in each of the chakras. Attention to diet and exercise are also helpful in raising the energy.

We can see that although it is important to be aware of our biological needs and human desires, we do not have to be the prisoner of the pleasure cult, inordinate desires, or our karmic interactions. We have free will to choose how we will relate to life and to redirect what we consider to be our lesser desires into higher expressions of God-desire for the fulfillment of the path of the ascension. In so doing, we may very well attract the perfect partner in life.

Ultimately, each of us must choose the path that works best for our own soul. All of us must have a path that we can follow, steps that are not too difficult—nor too easy. The initiations that are set for us are appropriate to our soul's attainment and progress on the path. If you feel that marriage is your calling but there isn't someone who you want to marry and who wants to marry you, follow the example of the saints and mystics and of unmarried people you admire.

Nurture friendships and involve yourself in serving and helping others. You can remember the verse in the Bible that says, "Thy Maker is thine husband,"[8] and you can find great comfort and fulfillment in a personal relationship with our God. Many great souls have lived on this earth and walked the Path alone—with the comfort of being "all-one" with their Higher Self and with God.

It may be a surprise to learn that the heaven-world is not so concerned whether you are married or not. The decision to marry can seem of such momentous import in the human scene. And yet to the angels and masters in heaven, human marriage is seen from a different perspective. They take a larger view, one that encompasses the total evolution of the soul.

What really matters is that you pass your tests in life and your initiations on the spiritual path. If the tests are passed as you are married, all well and good. If they are passed as you remain single and find your wholeness in your relationship with God, this is also well and good. Heaven is more concerned about your marriage to your divine spouse.

As you focus on discovering and fulfilling your special mission and pursuing your soul's divine destiny, trust that if it is your destiny to be married in this life, God will connect you with the one you are supposed to meet.

4
Sacred Energy

Love must be as much a light as it is a flame.

Henry David Thoreau

The Purpose of Sexual Union

There is an exchange of energy during sexual intercourse. There is a connection, chakra to chakra. Energy is released during orgasm and energy is moving not only physically but also spiritually.

The union of Alpha and Omega, the masculine and feminine principles, is the basic principle of creation. This may manifest in new life, the conception of children. It may also manifest as creativity in many other forms as the exchange of sacred energy brings balance of masculine and feminine energies in man and woman.

Sexual union between two people sharing their love and commitment is intended to be adoration of the God within one another. The love exchanged also determines the action and interchange of energies. The welling up of love within husband and wife helps to bring everything else into divine order within their relationship.

The institution of marriage and the blessing of a marriage by a representative of God provides a spiritual forcefield and a circle of protection for the love between man and woman. Without that blessing, the physical union between man and woman does not have the same protection, and loss of light through the base chakra is one concern for those who become involved in sexual union outside of marriage. This is especially the case if one of the partners has more light in the aura than the other—the one with more light has more to lose. For those who become involved with multiple partners, the consequences are multiplied.

On a spiritual level, there is also an exchange of energies at the level of the electronic belt. You take on or take within you a little piece of everyone you sleep with, even as you give them a little piece of yourself. Even more, you take in a little piece of every person they have slept with, as these energies are in their electronic belt and aura. That is one reason why many people today have a sense of confusion about love and relationships. They literally have a whirlpool of energy inside of them through all of the different relationships they have partaken of.

At the same time, they have given parts of themselves to other people. Some who have been promiscuous, especially at an early age, say that they almost don't know who they are any more. And the more they seek love through sexual union, the more disconnected they become from their soul and inner identity and the more confused they become.[1]

What actually occurs during intercourse is the descent of the Kundalini energy. The energies of the upper chakras (Spirit) descend to the lower chakras and the energy is released in the base chakra (Matter). Some of this energy is intended to rise again. Ideally, at the conclusion of intercourse, the energy of the Mother light rises and then waters the upper chakras, going up through the crown in the pattern of the shepherd's crook to anchor in the third-eye chakra.

When the energies are drawn back there through silent meditation on the third eye, what has now happened is that the energies have descended and risen. They have gone a complete circle and the whole body is nourished with the sacred fire. If the energy does not rise again, it continues to rest in the lower chakras and there is a less than complete spiritual fulfillment.

Each chakra has its purpose according to the original divine plan. The upper chakras are the centers that focus the energies of Spirit in the body. The lower chakras are the centers of Matter (think of the Latin *mater*, "mother"). The throat chakra is the center that has the greatest power. It is the center of the first ray, and its intended use is for speech, for prayer and affirmation, for praising God and uplifting our fellow man. It carries the power of creation through the spoken Word.

The blessing of a marriage by a representative of God provides a spiritual forcefield and a circle of protection for the love between man and woman.

Viewed energetically, when the throat chakra is placed in proximity with the base chakra in oral sex, there is a juxtaposition of the upper chakras with the lower chakras in an inverted position at a time when the sacred energies are being released for the purposes of creation. This induces a downward spiral of the light that is opposite to the natural flow of energy in the body. It is the reverse of the ascension current.

In oral sex, the light goes to the lower chakras for the sexual experience but it is not raised again afterwards. And the more this is practiced, the less the Kundalini rises between times, until you find that the energies become centered largely in the lower chakras. As this practice continues, it leads to a greater physicality in the experience of sex, which can become an addiction in some people.

While sexual energy is flowing in oral sex and there is the

physical experience of sexual release, there is not the spiritual interchange that should occur. Over time, this lowering of the light and the loss of the life-force can result in the loss of opportunity for the soul to attain the ascension—unless the practice is forsaken and the violet flame is used to transmute this energy misused.

The sacred fire in the base chakra is given to us for procreation and for the balance of masculine-feminine energies in man and woman. It is intended to be used for the creation of good works to the glory of God. It is a portion of the Divine that our loving Father-Mother God have bestowed upon us.

The sacred fire in the base-of-the-spine chakra is a portion of the Divine that our loving Father-Mother God have bestowed upon us. It is intended to be used for the creation of good works to the glory of God.

If we spend our spiritual energy prematurely or unwisely, that energy is no longer available to be raised up the spinal altar. We miss out on the blessing and wholeness that come from the nourishing of the higher chakras and the opening of the crown and the third eye for wisdom, illumination and divine vision.

In contrast, when you raise the sacred fire of the Kundalini and you experience the bliss of God and the entering into your God Presence, this can be a far greater experience than the mere exchange of sexual energies. You then will naturally come to place more emphasis upon the union with God and less emphasis on the sexual experience, and you will achieve the balance in your life that you, by free will, wish to have.

This is why the love that is expressed by couples may change over time. The intensity of the love of a young couple in the throes of their first passion may gradually give way to a deepening and more mature love that is more sacrificial and yet every bit as tender and caring.

So it becomes a question of priorities. All the energy you raise goes to your ascension. At the same time, it is important that some of us bring forth children, and this is a natural and normal desire—and for most people, a part of their divine plan. The fruit of the union of man and woman may also appear in other forms as their joint service to the world. So heaven gives us the opportunity to love and to evolve together.

Choices in Life

We all have choices to make each day as to where we will place our attention and how we will use our energy. The choices we make regarding relationships are among the most profound and far-reaching of any we make in life.

There are many factors that influence these decisions. We would hope to be led unfailingly by the inner voice and an awareness of the divine plan for our life. Unfortunately, there are also other forces that seek to influence us.

We have our own momentums and habits from the past. If we have good momentums, then we are blessed and it will be easier to make good choices. If we have negative momentums from this or past lives, then we have work to do to change these habits, transmute the karma associated with them, and give ourselves a clean slate on which to write a new story.

We will also deal with the part of us that perhaps would like to follow a lesser road—the not-self or the dweller-on-the-threshold. This part seeks the way that is easy in the moment—a temporary pleasure or indulgence that undermines our mission and the destiny held for us by our Higher Self. Just as importantly, we will deal with external forces wanting us to follow their lead.

Movies, television, music and popular culture paint a

picture of sex and relationships that is often far from the reality of life—and even further from what life is intended to be. When these images are before us all the time, it is easy to begin to think that what is portrayed on the screen is normal, even when our calling in life may be very different.

Those around us also hold expectations of what we should do. For teenagers it is usually called peer pressure: "Everyone is doing it. What's wrong with you?" But at any age, even well-meaning family or friends sometimes try to push us into relationships and experiences that would not be our own inner choice.

Movies, television, music and popular culture paint a picture of sex and relationships that is often far from what life is intended to be.

The key to dealing with this is to know yourself, know what you want for your life, and think about the consequences of your choices. We hope that this book will give you knowledge that will help you make choices based on a deeper understanding of yourself at a spiritual level. We also hope that you will have a greater understanding of how the choices you make now will affect your ability to find what you really want in life in years to come.

Think about the path you wish to pursue and make a commitment to follow it. There will be many circumstances in life that could potentially take you from that path. It is a good idea not to wait until a challenge to your chosen path arises to decide what you are going to do. When the car is about to crash, it is too late to think about putting your seatbelt on.

Be prepared before a situation arises where you might face a temptation. What will you do? Make a plan and be specific. Then, if the situation does arise, you already know what to do.

You don't have to figure it out in the midst of intense emotions or external pressure.

If you want to follow a different path from the one portrayed by the world and popular culture, if you want to hold sex and relationships as something sacred, and not just for pleasure, then it will take some effort to swim against the tide.

Think about what will make you happier in the end. Would you rather look back on your life and see that you did what other people wanted you to do? Or would you prefer to look back and see that you were true to yourself and your own higher calling?

Think also about which path is more likely to attract the person you are searching for. Who do you want to be with? Someone who simply follows the crowd, or someone who is true to his own heart and soul, someone who knows her own destined path and has the courage to follow it?

Unwanted Attention

Beyond peer pressure and the influences we are all aware of in our lives, there are also unseen forces. Because they are unseen, we are often unaware of them, but they may be the very things that trip us up simply because we are not prepared.

One thing we all may face from time to time is unwanted attention. When a person is not in full control of the energy of the base-of-the-spine chakra, this energy seeks an outlet and it may begin to be channeled in unhealthy directions. A person with this problem may become fixated upon a member of the opposite sex. They may think of this person all the time—perhaps in a sexual way or perhaps in some sort of romantic fantasy. They may even see the person in their dreams. All the while they are feeding energy into this fantasy, and the energy continues to build.

This replaying of thoughts, images and feelings creates a negative spiral in the aura, and each time the person replays the mental image or the fantasy, it forms another turn of the spiral. Like an electromagnet, the more turns, the more intense the energy becomes. The person may think he (or she) is in love. If he knows about these concepts, he may even fantasize that he has found his soul mate or twin flame. All the while, energy of the base chakra is fed into the spiral. And this energy is transferred to the victim over the arc of attention from the one who is caught up in this fantasy.

This can become a considerable weight upon the recipient, even if nothing is said or done physically. The effects may manifest in all kinds of ways—sleeplessness, a feeling of depression or a weight upon the heart, problems with their own sexuality or control of the energy of the base chakra.

If unchecked, the energy of infatuation can build to the point where the person who began with a choice to engage in seemingly innocent fantasy or daydreaming now has little control over the energy spiral that has been created. As in the story of the sorcerer's apprentice, once the energy spiral has been set in motion, it can take on a life of its own. There is no turning back, or so it seems. And if circumstances permit and the person on the receiving end also enters into the spiral, the two may find that they are swept up in an intensity of emotion that is bigger than both of them. They may have an affair, even if one or both are married.

People caught up in these situations may take no thought for their spouses or families or the effects on their children. They can be convinced that the feelings that they have are so compelling that they must be right. But once the spiral has been released and the energy dissipated (perhaps overnight, perhaps over days, weeks or months) they find there is nothing left to the relationship. The end result is only a loss of light, a loss of trust, betrayal of love and the devastation of a broken home.

Susan was assigned to work with William in her workplace and became aware of his attraction towards her. She was happily married, but she found herself thinking about him and falling into thoughts that took her where she did not want to go. She realized that these thoughts might not be her own and that they might be the result of William's energy of attraction impinging on her subconscious. She wanted none of it.

She decided to talk to her husband and tell him about this energy, to bring it out into the open. Her husband was understanding and sure of her love for him and his for her. He knew that nothing physical had taken place and there was not even any real attraction there, but he knew that Susan was not happy with the seemingly carefree banter and unwanted attention she was receiving at work.

They both understood that this was a test. William's actions had not crossed the line of sexual harassment, so they could not approach the situation from that angle. They also realized that William was probably not conscious of what he was doing and that it would not be appropriate or helpful to talk with him about it. That left spiritual solutions.

Susan and her husband prayed about the situation each night and placed it in God's hands. She observed her own energy and the energy coming from William and did not let herself get drawn into that spiral.

Within a short time the situation righted itself. She no longer felt any feelings towards William at all, and soon afterwards their work assignments were changed. A little while later, he left the company. She doesn't blame William for what happened, but believes he, himself, may have been the victim of unseen forces that sought to work against both of them.

The Burden of Sexual Fantasy

U nderstanding the energy of the base-of-the-spine chakra and how it can flow over the arc of a person's attention gives a whole new perspective on the concept of the sex goddess or pinup girl.

When a woman allows her image to be reproduced and circulated widely for the attention of thousands or millions of men, this image allows their imaginations to make an energetic connection with the one who is depicted. Their energy and focus of their attention can be felt as it goes out to the object of their fantasy. The same thing can happen to men. The movie star voted "sexiest man alive" in a popular magazine may not be aware of the energy he is dealing with from the attention of millions of women.

This may seem harmless, but the effects can be devastating. Many centerfolds, pinup girls, rock stars and pop culture icons have felt the burden of this energy. Marilyn Monroe is one example. She was the object of the sex fantasies of millions of men. It was so great a weight upon her that night after night she could not sleep, and she resorted to alcohol and sleeping pills to try to find some relief.

Some people believe her death was due to an accidental overdose of barbiturates, some believe it was suicide, others believe it was homicide. Whatever the outer cause, the spiritual record shows that the underlying burden was that she was suffering from the mass projections of millions through her posters, pictures and images in the movies.

This sad drama also points to the accountability we have in our own lives for what we do and how we present ourselves to the world. What types of images do we post of ourselves on Facebook, YouTube, Snapchat? What type of energy do they attract to us?

We can also think about the clothes we wear. Most of us want to be appealing and attractive in our appearance—but what is our benchmark for looking good? Are we trying to look "sexy"? If so, what energy will we have to deal with on the return current of people's attention on us? And is our appearance contributing to the discomfort of others, making it difficult for them to keep their own vows and commitments?

Instead of thinking about clothes as an attempt to meet the fashion standards of the world, we can think of them as a means to complement and enhance the light of the aura and the soul.

There is nothing wrong with trying to look good. But in the highest sense, clothing should reflect and complement our true self. Instead of thinking about clothes as an attempt to meet the fashion standards of the world, we can think of them as a means to complement and enhance the light of the aura and the soul. With this perspective, we can begin to feel some liberation from the burdens of trying to keep up with passing fashions.

Another helpful idea for avoiding unwanted attention is one my father gave me when I was younger. He told me not to allow members of the opposite sex to enter my bedroom, even briefly.

He explained that having seen the room where you sleep, it is then easier for even well-meaning friends to fantasize about you and think about you in your bedroom.

Even if they would not consciously do such a thing, their lesser self might try to project this on the screen of their mind, even while they are asleep. Better not to place a stone of stumbling in front of another. It is a kindness to others to help them avoid temptation, and it is a kindness to yourself, whether you are a man or a woman, to avoid arousing unwanted attention.

Teresa is a former prostitute who now understands these principles well. More than thirty years ago she ran a successful brothel in Louisiana. Then she "saw the light," as she describes it. She turned her life around, embraced Jesus Christ as her Lord and Savior, and completely forsook her old lifestyle. She decided to become celibate and to use the violet flame to balance the karma of misuse of the base chakra. She moved to New York and is a now a pillar in her community. A cheerful soul by nature, she assists others as best she can, serves in her local church and wears modest and attractive clothing.

Teresa says, "No one here even knows of my past, and I do not share it with them. It is as if it was a past life. I know that God has forgiven me, and I am very happy with my life as it is today. As a prostitute I thought I was tough, but I never slept well. Now I sleep like a baby."

Unseen Forces

These examples illustrate how the energy and attention of other people, even when unseen, can affect us. Beyond this, just as there are angels and masters who help and support us, there are also unseen forces of darkness that work against our highest goals.

These forces may be beings that dwell on the astral plane—a frequency of time and space beyond the physical, corresponding to the emotional body and the negative levels of the collective subconscious of humanity. These may be souls who have passed from the screen of life and did not have the means to navigate to the etheric, those higher planes of being that we think of as the heaven world.

They may also be malevolent spirits—fallen angels and their followers who have consciously turned to a path of darkness.[2] These dark beings have cut themselves off from the Source of light and energy that is God, so they can only sustain their existence by taking light from those in embodiment on earth. They would steal our light if we allow it. They try to get us to do things that will cause us to lose our light—to become angry or irritated, to use drugs or alcohol, or to misuse the light of the base chakra. If we engage in these things, we give them energy, and most of the time we are not even aware of it.

How do these unseen forces work? One means is to project

thoughts and feelings towards us. Suddenly a stray thought appears on the screen of our mind, seemingly out of nowhere. This projection may even be repeated over and over again, and we wonder why we are now thinking about something we know we don't really want to do.

This may be reinforced by the projection of a sense of unworthiness, continually try to remind us of episodes from the past that we regret or consider shameful. They try to tell us that we are sinners, we have done all these terrible things, and we may as well do them again. They try to make us discouraged and depressed about ourselves, to feel that we will never be free. Whether it is drugs, alcohol, misuses of the sacred fire or overeating, the strategy is the same.

The first step in dealing with these projections is to see them for what they are. We can learn to distinguish between our own thoughts and feelings and those that are projected at us by unseen forces.

Once we have recognized what is happening, the next step is to decide not to enter in to the energy, to disengage from it. The Master Morya once said, "You can't help it if a bird lands on your head, but you don't have to let him build a nest in your hair!"[3] It doesn't help if we indulge these projections by revolving them over and over in our own minds.

If we find ourselves beset by such projections, it is time, as the Bible says, to "put on the whole armor of God." We can fortify our minds and hearts with light so that we are not so receptive to astral projections. We can reconnect with the Higher Self through prayer, meditation, decrees, music—whatever will reestablish that tie. And we can call to angels of light to protect and strengthen us and to deal with the forces of darkness.

If we find ourselves falling into self-condemnation, we can remind ourselves that we are sons and daughters of God and he has provided forgiveness for us. We don't have to accept a sense of worthlessness. If we are sorry for our mistakes, if we have asked for forgiveness and decided we no longer want to make the same mistakes again, then we can be free and whole before God.

Sometimes we are vulnerable to these forces when we don't have the full strength of our physical body—whether through fatigue, not eating well, or a physical problem such as illness. These are times to increase our spiritual practices for the sealing and protection of the aura. We can also ask others to pray for us.

Another time when we may be vulnerable to astral forces is in the transition to sleep and in the dream state. During sleep the soul leaves the body and is free to travel in other realms. Ideally we should journey to the highest octaves of light, visiting etheric cities and the retreats of the masters,[4] but sometimes the soul rises no higher than the astral plane.

If we find ourselves in these realms, we may encounter astral beings there who seek to take our light, whether through projections of fear in nightmares or projections of sexual thoughts and scenarios culminating in a physical release. Beings of the astral plane may even assume the mask and the persona of individuals we have known in this embodiment or in the past. We think we are dreaming of a person we have known when it is actually an astral entity trying to impose itself upon us. Their goal is to take the light of the chakras.

If you find yourself facing this challenge or have difficulty sleeping, remember that where you place your attention and energy before you go to sleep can make a difference in where you end up in consciousness when you are out of the body. For example, if you watch a horror movie before you sleep, you may well have nightmares and other experiences on the astral plane. If you place your attention on a spiritual teaching or engage in a period of prayer or meditation before retiring, you can more easily reach higher planes. Avoiding heavy food for a few hours before sleep can also be helpful.

If you call to them, the angels will also assist. Offer a prayer to the angels to guard you while you sleep and escort your soul to octaves of light and the retreats of the masters. Many people find that a period of prayer, meditation or mantras in the evening puts them in a level of awareness where they have uplifting spiritual experiences on the etheric plane while they sleep. Even if they do not remember everything that occurred, they return the next morning with a sense of being spiritually recharged and prepared for the challenges of the day.

Whether in the day or in the night, you don't have to allow negative forces into your life. You have a mighty I AM Presence. The angels will defend you if you invoke them. There is a peace that comes when you are no longer the victim of unseen forces, when you are in control of your energies and your life.

"Male and Female ..."

The Book of Genesis records that "In the beginning, God created the heaven and the earth." On the sixth day (the sixth cycle of the unfoldment of creation) God said, "Let us make man in our image, after our likeness." And thus it is recorded, "Male and female created he them."[5]

We see in this allegorical account that God is possessed of a divine polarity, both masculine and feminine. We may think of God as He, as God has long been known in the West. Spiritually this reflects the understanding that God as Spirit is in polarity with his creation and the entire matter universe. But within that divine One, that androgynous being, God is both male and female, masculine and feminine—something that has long been known in the East. In fact, God is both Father and Mother to us all.

When our twin flames were sent forth to experience life on earth, they were endowed with a 60-40 ratio of the attributes of this divine polarity that is God's nature. The one who would embody the masculine aspect was endowed with 60 percent masculine attributes and 40 percent feminine, while the one who would embody the feminine aspect was endowed with 60 percent feminine attributes and 40 percent masculine. It is this imbalance that creates the desire for oneness with one's counterpart, that impels man and woman to search for their twin flame.

This polarity also allows souls to experience different attributes of God in different embodiments. In a masculine embodiment, the soul has the opportunity to expand the masculine qualities of God, and in a feminine embodiment, the soul learns to develop the feminine qualities. In order for each twin flame to maintain balance in their causal body and also to facilitate the balancing of karma and gaining new experience, twin flames will be assigned different polarities in the span of their soul evolution.

Unfortunately, individuals sometimes find it difficult to adjust to this change in roles. Rather than entering fully into the new polarity and developing the qualities that will bring balance to their soul, they may try to hold on to what may be more familiar from past embodiments. Women may try to assume a more masculine way of life and men may tend more toward the feminine. When these tendencies to go against one's karma and destined role in life are unchecked, they may take the form of homosexuality.

Elizabeth Clare Prophet explains the spiritual significance of this departure from the divine plan of man and woman and its effects on soul evolution:

With each incarnation, male or female, we are given a certain charge at the base-of-the-spine chakra. There are three energies that rise in the Kundalini—the *ida*, *pingala* and *sushumna*.[6]... If a male chooses to engage in the practice of homosexuality, he will pervert the masculine ray of those three, the Alpha current. If it is misused continually, he will be depleted of that masculine ray, and this often produces an effeminate nature. If a female chooses to engage in the practice of lesbianism, she will misuse the feminine aspect, or the Omega spiral, of self. This deprives the person of the fullness of the feminine potential. It may cause a shift over into a less intuitive and less exalted state.[7]

The practices of homosexuality are therefore in opposition to the natural flow of the life-force in man and woman. Individuals thereby misuse the sacred fire, the Kundalini, the flame of life, and they also lose the balance of the Alpha-Omega polarity within them and between them and their twin flame. The longer this path is followed, the greater the imbalance becomes, and it becomes increasingly difficult to break the pattern with each successive embodiment in which it is practiced. When people choose this way, they are creating an imbalance in the spiritual forces within them, and if their goal is the resurrection and the ascension, they will need to rebalance their energies.

The raising of the Kundalini and the balancing of the chakras is the primary goal of seekers on the path to God. In the practice of same-sex union, there is the lowering of the energies of the sacred fire. It is a misdirected attempt to find the wholeness that can come only through the divine union of masculine and feminine polarities, and in an attempt to reach that receding goal, there is often a focus on intensifying the physical experience of sex. Following that path can only lead the soul further from the God Presence and further from the true divine love the soul is seeking, the twin flame.

Many people say that one can abstain but one cannot change one's nature. It is true that energies that flow within us carve deep river beds. When we habitually express a particular use of sexual energy, we are carving a pattern within us, and our energy tends to keep flowing in the channel we have created.

Some people feel that they were born homosexual, and in one sense this may be true. If they have followed this path for a number of lifetimes, it may feel very familiar and natural. But if we look to the origin of the soul in the heart of God, it was not so—twin flames, the two halves of the divine whole, were created "male and female."

Somewhere in the evolution of the soul, a choice was made to follow a different path. A new momentum was built that was different from the original aspiration of the soul. Thus we see that change is possible, even if it may not happen overnight.[8] It takes time to close off one channel and open up another. So we must be patient with ourselves and others, never condemn, and place our focus on our own striving on the path of self-mastery.

We can use the violet flame and the science of the spoken Word to help change the course of the river and to create new channels for the flow of the energies of life. We can fill in the old riverbeds with violet flame. We can raise our energies in the service of life and find true wholeness within.

One's sex at birth is never by chance. It is always an opportunity for the soul to gain needed balance in the expression of the inner blueprint. The fulfillment of our mission and spiritual purpose in life comes through playing the role God has given us. There is a sanctity to the offices of father, mother, son, daughter, brother, sister, husband, wife. If we have a feminine embodiment, for example, then we play the role of mother, daughter, sister, wife. If we are male, we play the role of father, son, brother, husband. Whatever our role, we should concentrate on being the best that we can be in that role.

Max is someone who changed the course of the river. With a lifelong addiction to sex and a history of homosexuality, he never thought he could change. But then he found the violet flame.

Skeptical at first, he began to try it. He observed changes in his life over a period of months. It became easier to say no to a lifestyle of promiscuity that he knew was destructive for him. He drifted away from some of his friends when they were not supportive of his choice. He got some excellent counseling from a gifted therapist and took up a spiritual path that has made a difference in his life.

"I now know a greater contentment than I have ever known," Max says. "Although it was not an easy road and I did not always get it right, I do feel that life is once again a joy for me. I really feel that God and the violet flame changed the course of the river of life that is flowing through me."

Freedom through Forgiveness

One reason why projections of condemnation seem to enter our world so easily is that that we have within us elements of self-condemnation. The external condemnation ties into and activates a negative pattern that is already there. The same is true of any negative projection. If we have something inside us that resonates with it, we are more likely to identify with it and allow it to enter.

When Jesus said, "The prince of this world cometh, and hath nothing in me,"[9] he knew what he was talking about. He had already cleaned up his inner world. He had no points of vulnerability. We can aspire to this also, and one of the greatest spiritual tools to get there is the violet flame. We can send it into our past misuses of the light and see them consumed.

God does not hold our mistakes before us. In fact, he does not acknowledge our errors, because in his consciousness, they were long ago consumed by the violet flame. The devil, on the other hand, will never forgive or forget. He will hold up our supposed sins even in the moment we are ascending. The forces of darkness try to make life *too* serious. They try to make the deep, dark past some kind of enormous problem, and they whisper to us that we can never overcome it.

We all have karma and we all have shortcomings—otherwise we wouldn't still be here on earth. It is important to have a realistic assessment of ourselves, to have a sense of what will be needed to balance and transmute that karma. At the same time, we can be joyous in the midst of that process as we ask for forgiveness, call forth the violet flame and move out of the shadows into the light.

We can only be tormented by our past if we allow it to torment us. The past is not real. Only eternal life is real. Time and space are where we experience the effects of our karma. Only in time does death exist, and it is our perception of time and space that limits us.

We can triumph over time and space, and that triumph is over the matrix of limitation. In truth, we are already eternal, immortal, infinite beings of light. We just have to recognize it and become who we truly are.

Protecting Your Aura

An important spiritual key for dealing with projections of negativity, whether they come from people around you or from unseen forces, is to seal and protect the aura.

One effective means to do this is to invoke the tube of light. This is shown in the Chart of Your Divine Self as the cylinder of white light descending from your I AM Presence (see page 55).

To establish this tube of light around you, visualize your I AM Presence above you and see a waterfall of light descending from that Presence all around you, nine feet in diameter. Once you have this image in your mind, you can reinforce it by giving the following decree three times or more:

> Beloved I AM Presence bright,
> Round me seal your tube of light
> From ascended master flame
> Called forth now in God's own name.
> Let it keep my temple free
> From all discord sent to me.
>
> I AM calling forth violet fire
> To blaze and transmute all desire,
> Keeping on in freedom's name
> Till I AM one with the violet flame.

The tube of light seals and protects your aura, your mind, your thoughts and feelings. It is as strong and impenetrable as you visualize and invoke it.

Also available to assist us are the angels God has sent to heal and protect us. Archangel Michael is the leader of the angels of protection. He and his legions of angels can seal you from unwanted attention and unseen forces. He can establish a forcefield of protective blue light around you in answer to your prayer. The angels want to help you, and they can do so more effectively if you call to them and work with them.

Here is a quick prayer you can use in an emergency:

Archangel Michael,
Help me! Help me! Help me!

You can call to Archangel Michael daily using the following decree before traveling or at any time you feel the need for protection:

Lord Michael before,
Lord Michael behind,
Lord Michael to the right,
Lord Michael to the left,
Lord Michael above, Lord Michael below,
Lord Michael, Lord Michael wherever I go!

I AM his love protecting here!
I AM his love protecting here!
I AM his love protecting here!

Marion is a seventy-two-year-old widow who swears by this prayer. She first gave it when her husband passed on and she was afraid to be alone at night. Now she starts each day calling to Archangel Michael. The love and companionship she feels from this great archangel are a constant comfort in her life.

If you get to know Archangel Michael, you will find that he is the best friend you could have. He can protect you and your loved ones and all of your relationships in this life. He can protect the reunion of twin flames and expose those who would come as impostors or imitators of that light.

See Chapter 8 for additional spiritual exercises to seal and protect your spiritual path.

5
A Love Worth
Waiting For

Painful as it might be, beloved ones, I tell you,
you are separated from your twin flame for
one reason and one alone: You have not loved
one another as Christ has loved you individ-
ually, and therefore the karma has produced
the separation.

CHAMUEL AND CHARITY
ARCHANGELS OF LOVE

Wanting to Be Pure

have spoken with many teenagers, and adults as well, who have told me that they want to return to a state of purity they once knew. Others have spoken about being a technical virgin but not feeling pure. They all wanted to attract to themselves the one who was right for them and they wanted to lead a life of purity once more.

This is truly what it means to be a virgin. The virgin consciousness is not so much about the physical body. Virginity is not a condition of the flesh alone—it is most importantly a state of the mind and the heart, the soul and the spirit.

Regardless of your past, you can change your present and your future. You can begin right now to manifest the love that you long to attract. For you do have opportunity and choices as to how you will spend God's light and energy that is given to you each day.

The decision to be sexually active outside of marriage can be seen from the spiritual perspective as an equation of energy. Each day we are given a certain allotment of energy and we have only so much energy to spend.

How much loss of light is too much?

How much loss before we no longer have the spiritual light to fulfill our mission?

How much loss before we no longer have the inner magnet to attract the One we are seeking?

These are questions that bear prayerful thought, for the consequences of our choices may be far reaching.

Waiting for the One

I t has been said that a love worth having is a love worth wait-ing for. It seems a simple concept—almost self-evident—but much of our popular culture seems to argue against it.

In the midst of the sexual revolution of the 1970s, there was a popular song that advised, "If you can't be with the one you love, love the one you're with."[1] Many people seem to live this way. Rather than waiting for the one they know they are meant to be with, they settle for the love that is available. The song seems to be a call for liberation and more love—but what is the cost?

If you haven't already found the one you are meant to be with, think about that person—your twin flame, your soul mate, the destined love of your life. Would you hope that they are in a relationship with someone else, since they haven't found you yet? Or would you hope that they might be waiting for you?

Now imagine you are that twin flame or soul mate. What would you be looking for? If you were walking down the road and you saw yourself standing there, would you stop? Would this wonderful person you are imagining be interested in you as you are today?

In romance, as in other relationships in life, we tend to at-tract who we are. Like attracts like. And if we want to attract the perfect love, a soul with light, then that is what we need to become. We can work to amplify the love and light within us. We should think in terms of scrubbing off our karma and becoming the best possible person we can be in order to attract the best possible partner in life.

This may take time, and patience may be needed. We may find that we have to forego some things we would like to do, that might feel good in the moment. If we want to keep and build the light that is the magnet to attract the person we are really searching for, we may need to make some sacrifices. But these will seem insignificant in the long run. The difference in having the right partner in life can be almost beyond calculation.

The Search for Love

In the quest for the One we are intended to be with, there is spiritual work to do. But what are the practical steps to take? How do you actually go about finding the right person?

The usual answer is dating—meet a lot of people, go on dates, improve your relationship skills and eventually you will find someone. This may work for some people. However, on the spiritual path, relationships take on a different perspective. It is not merely a matter of finding someone you are attracted to, that you might be *happy* with. The aim is to find the person you are *meant* to be with for the fulfillment of your life plan and for your spiritual growth. And of course, this is what will bring the deepest love and most long-lasting happiness in the end.

There is also the question of where you want to put your focus. Romantic relationships take time and energy, and you have a finite amount of both in this lifetime.

Many people spend years moving from relationship to relationship. They may know that their current boyfriend/girlfriend is not someone they want to spend the rest of their life with, but the relationship is fulfilling for now and meets a need. But what is the net gain from the experience, and what opportunities are lost?

Not long after I graduated from medical school, I met a doctor from England who was visiting the hospital where I worked in Australia. He was a plastic surgeon and I was a trainee anesthetist. We had the same sense of humor, really liked each other and seemed to hit it off well. I had already planned to visit England to do further training in my field when he left after a couple of weeks to return home. He gave me his address and told me to look him up when I got there.

After I was settled in my small flat in Hull, in the north of England, I drove down to Cambridge to visit him. I pulled my car up outside the city and thought about the situation. Did I really want to meet him? Where would this lead?

If you find yourself attracted to someone, before you do anything, it is always safe to do the spiritual work and use the violet flame. Wait for the inner voice that will give unerring guidance.

I was feeling uneasy. I prayed and decided that it did not feel right. Although there was a real attraction on both sides, my heart told me not to proceed. It might be fun or enjoyable, but I had the sense that he was not the one for me. I started the car, turned around and drove back home.

I do not know what would have happened if I had taken the other fork in the road. I might have found out very quickly that the relationship was not right—or perhaps it would have been a wide cycle of ten or twenty years or more.

From where I am now, I can see that the road not taken was the road that was not meant for me to take. God had other plans for me, and fortunately I stopped, looked, listened and was obedient to the inner voice.

It is important to remember that there is a plan for your life. It includes everything that you need for your soul's growth and your victory, including the right person to be with.

If you find yourself attracted to someone, before you do anything, it is always safe to do the spiritual work and use the violet flame. Don't make decisions based on the intensity of emotions, but wait for the inner voice—the still, small voice within that will give unerring guidance.

If you wait, you may well find that an intense attraction you feel for someone dissipates. If you use the violet flame and the energy of karma has been transmuted, you may wonder what you ever saw in the person. You may be very glad that you avoided a karmic entanglement and another unnecessary sexual liaison—and possibly the creation of a whole new round of karma. You kept your light and your energy to magnetize the true relationship that God and your Higher Self have planned for you in this life.

On the other hand, it may be that the relationship is the one that is intended for you. In this case the spiritual work will only enhance it. This relationship may be with your twin flame or a soul mate, or it may be a relationship of karma that needs to be resolved in a very personal way. In one sense, it does not matter. Whatever relationship is ordained for you will provide the greatest opportunity to give and receive love, to experience your divine potential and to make progress on the path.

My grandmother used to say, "What's for you won't go past you." It doesn't hurt to "delay and pray."

God will let you know if a particular relationship is right—if you give him the opportunity to tell you. However, if you don't want to know because you want this person or a relationship more than you want the Truth, God will respect your free-will choice. And you may find yourself learning in the school of hard knocks.

Letting God Lead

Two thousand years ago, Jesus made a promise to his disciples: "Seek ye first the kingdom of God, and his righteousness, and *all* these things will be added unto you."[2] This is true in relationships as it is in every other area of life.

Many people on the spiritual path have discovered that they only found the right person when they gave up their own efforts and put the search in God's hands. Often this took a leap of faith. Sometimes the decision was born of a kind of desperation after their own attempts ended badly.

This was true for me. Even before I knew there was such a thing as a twin flame, I was always looking for the one I was supposed to be with. I dated dozens of people in my medical school days and later as a young doctor. Each time I was disappointed. Some of them were very fine people, young doctors or other professionals with wonderful futures ahead of them. But I usually discovered very quickly that they weren't the one for me.

Finally, after more than a dozen years of searching, I found someone I thought could be the one I was supposed to marry. Steven was a professional person. We were both committed to the spiritual path. Everything looked great on the surface. I wanted to get married and he wanted to marry me. I liked him, so I convinced myself it was love. We became engaged and the marriage date was set. Invitations were sent out and all the arrangements for the ceremony were ready.

Then, suddenly, two weeks before the date, there was what I can only call a divine intercession. It was like a veil was lifted. Suddenly, I could see clearly. I realized that Steven was absolutely not the right person for me. I called the whole thing off.

I also realized from this experience that I really wasn't capable of finding the right person if I relied on my own outer mind. I decided to set aside my search. Weary of the merry-go-round I had put myself on, I had a period of several years not dating anyone. I concentrated on my spiritual path and my relationship with God, and I prayed for him to send the right person to me—on his timetable. I placed the entire matter of who I was supposed to marry in God's hands, and I found a peace about relationships that I had not known before.

At the right time, God brought me to Peter, my future husband, and made it very clear that he was the one. Peter had also set aside dating a number of years earlier in order to single-mindedly pursue his spiritual path. At the age of thirty-three, he had felt that he was ready, and he offered a very heartfelt prayer that if it was the will of God, he might find someone to be loved by and to love. Then he let the prayer go, also leaving it in God's hands.

When we met a few months after this, it wasn't a matter of falling in love—that came a little later. It was more like a flash of recognition and illumination. We both knew, on an instant, that we were supposed to be together. There was no outer sign, just an inner knowing. It was like a veil was lifted, and this time I was looking at reality, not unreality.

I doubt I would have found Peter if I had pursued my previous course. We had first met a few years earlier at a conference in America, and we shared a common bond as fellow Australians. We had a few conversations, but nothing more than that, and at the time I made the decision to surrender my search, we lived on different continents, half a world apart. But when I put God in charge, it seemed that he rearranged my whole life to bring us together.

For such a decision to work, it needs to come from a place deep inside. It can't be an attempt to bargain with God. It has to be founded on faith—faith that God is fully capable of bringing the right person to us and that the love will be there. We may even need to get past the fear that God might saddle us with a person that we don't really like or love—like a bad arranged marriage. (And perhaps we have subconscious memories of such negative experiences from past lives.)

The decision can only come from a place of true surrender and a willingness to let go of our outer desires and the programming of family, the media and society. But this is not a surrender to an impersonal God outside of oneself, but a surrender to one's own Real Self—being willing to let go of the lesser self so that the greater Self can enter and direct one's life.

If you are searching for your twin flame, this may be the only way to reach that goal. Your lesser self has made karma that separated you from your Higher Self and your twin flame. You are already one with your twin flame at the level of your Higher Self, and it may be that only by allowing that Higher Self to direct your life could you ever be reunited on the outer.

One Christian couple write about the joy and fulfillment that come from doing just this. They call it "letting God write your love story."[3] Perhaps not everyone is ready to take this step. But if you are willing to make the leap of faith, you may find, as many others have, a new peace about relationships. You may also find that at the right time, God will find an amazing way to place you nose-to-nose with the one who is meant for you.

Dating

Letting go of the search doesn't mean locking yourself in a room and living like a monk or a nun. It may well mean setting aside the dating scene for a while. It may mean not living up to the expectations of friends or family that you should have a boyfriend/girlfriend right now.

The concept of dating as we know it today is quite a recent invention. A century or two ago, young people had friendships with members of the opposite sex, but to pursue a special or exclusive relationship with one person was expected to be based on a genuine interest in commitment and marriage.

The twentieth century brought a new freedom to pursue relationships—a liberation from marriages dictated by families or by social norms. People were more free to follow their hearts and pursue true love, but there have been some unfortunate side-effects. One of these is the negative aspects of dating that we see today.

Teenagers seem to start dating at ever younger ages, long before they are ready for or even thinking about commitment or marriage. Having a boyfriend or girlfriend is a goal in itself, and these relationships are not expected to last. The primary purpose is the excitement of romance and intimacy—whether that intimacy is just on an emotional level or whether it becomes physical as well.

These experiences may be enjoyable, but as young people go from one relationship to another, they often give a portion of themselves to each new partner. Through painful experience they often find that the other person was not able to hold that gift and honor it as they had hoped.

Some find that they are never again able to trust so completely or to fall in love so deeply. Emotional scars may take many years to heal. Sometimes they linger for a lifetime, along with AIDS, herpes or other diseases contracted when premature intimacy becomes physical.

In later years, when people could make the kind of commitment that marriage and an enduring relationship require, they have become accustomed to dating as the end point of relationships. Their needs for friendship and emotional (and even physical) intimacy are met through dating, and even though they might feel that something is missing, they have become accustomed to short-term, limited-commitment relationships. Sometimes they find themselves fearful or not knowing how to make the commitment or sacrifice necessary to have something more.

There is a spiritual price that is paid when people get stuck in what some have called "dating limbo." They never fully engage those portions of their life plan or karmic assignments that are intended to be fulfilled through marriage and family. We read the stories of those, especially women, who have led seemingly interesting and successful lives and then arrive in middle age with the realization that opportunities for marriage and family have passed them by.

Perhaps they had relationships along the way. But there is a great sense of regret at opportunities missed, including the opportunity to have children. Beyond this, the sense of loss may be a symptom of an idling of the spiritual growth of the soul, which has been sacrificed for the achievement of outer success.

Rounds of dating may also set up unrealistic expectations for relationships. When the excitement of romance fades and things get difficult, people have become accustomed to ending a relationship and moving on. They may find it difficult to get beyond being "in love with love" to discover a love that springs from a source that is deeper than romantic feelings and attractions.

The time of being single is often not valued as it should be. It provides unique opportunities for education, for spiritual growth, for single-minded dedication to the mission of the soul and the spiritual path. It is exemplified in the story of the teenager Jesus joining a caravan for India and his quest to find the great spiritual teachers of the East.[4] It is the story of the knights of the Round Table and their quest to slay dragons, set right the ills of the world and find the Holy Grail.

There is a tremendous idealism and energy of youth—and of those of any age who are alone with God—a yearning that finds its highest fulfillment in service to the world and oneness with God. If this energy is channeled prematurely or exclusively into relationships, people often deprive themselves of the greatest gifts of this stage in life.

There is a purpose for dating. It is a period of getting to know someone before deciding whether to make a commitment to a deeper relationship. If there is something about a person you can't live with, it is far better to find out before the marriage than after.

But before we talk more about dating and romance, let's look at something that is even more fundamental.

Friendship

I n the best of marriages, lovers are also friends. Friendship is a different kind of relationship from romance. It may not be as intense, but it is more enduring.

Friendship is about common interests, shared values and goals. A romantic relationship is more inward focused, more about the relationship itself and the other person. We tend to think of lovers seeking privacy, whereas friends welcome others to join their circle. C. S. Lewis describes the difference in this way: "We picture lovers face to face but Friends side by side; their eyes looking ahead."[5]

One difficulty with the modern emphasis on dating is that it tends to prematurely bypass the opportunity for friendship. It encourages people to ask whether there is an attraction before finding out if they have anything in common. It can lead to a superficial intimacy based on romantic feelings. Without a foundation of friendship, these relationships often last only as long as the feelings last.

The concept of a "date" also carries quite a bit of baggage. Sometimes dating can be stressful. Girls may spend hours choosing what to wear, getting their hair and makeup just right. Guys try just as hard, but they tend to focus more of their energy on what to say and do to get an emotional response.

The extent to which this can go is seen in books for women

like *How to Make a Man Fall in Love with You* and *How to Get Any Man to Do Anything You Want!* and how-to books for men like *The Game* and *How to Pick Up Girls*. The latter includes everything you need to know "from the most brilliantly disarming pick-up lines to long-term strategies for getting the most attractive, sensuous women around to fall in love with you."

Joshua Harris, author of *I Kissed Dating Goodbye*, tells the story of one young man whose strategy was to take a date to a furniture store. As they wandered the aisles he would ask her what tables and couches she would like in her home some day. "Girls go nuts for this," the young man said. He explained that with thoughts of marriage and family on their minds, girls would be more romantic and affectionate later in the evening.[6]

Love does not consist in gazing at each other but in looking outward together in the same direction.

ANTOINE DE SAINT EXUPÉRY

At the lowest level, there is often a lot of manipulation that goes on in dating. Some people are in the game for what they can get out of it, and they know how to push the emotional buttons of the opposite sex to get what they want.

But even with good intentions and no desire to manipulate others, people on a date usually try hard to look good and come across well. They genuinely want the other person to have a good time and they don't want to be rejected.

This can create an artificial environment, similar in some ways to a job interview. People may present very well initially, and you may not find out what a person is really like for quite some time. In the meantime you may have fallen in love with the image you see, more than with the real person. And by then, an emotional intensity may have built that makes it difficult to assess things objectively. You are already hooked. You may find yourself in a relationship that is not right or going through a painful process of emotional separation from a relationship that is not what you thought it was in the first place.

So if you meet someone you would like to get to know better, think about friendship first, before a romantic relationship. Many people find that group activities are a liberating alternative to dating. Whether in structured settings in organized groups or just friends enjoying activities together, there are many opportunities for recreation and social interaction with people of both sexes on the basis of friendship and mutual interests—without the emotional pressures and expectations of the one-on-one relationship. If the setting involves volunteer work or service to others, there is the added benefit of opportunities for personal and spiritual growth.

If you are meeting someone in a group setting, don't spend all your time with that person. See how they interact with other people as well as you. Do they treat other people with respect and kindness? Are they trying to impress other people? Or are they real? How do they cope with stress and challenges? How do they treat their parents?

A friendship is something that develops naturally. Lewis continues:

> The very condition of having Friends is that we should want something else besides Friends. Where the truthful answer to the question *Do you see the same truth?* would be "I see nothing and I don't care about the truth;

I only want a Friend," no friendship can arise—though Affection of course may. There would be nothing for the Friendship to be *about*; and Friendship must be about something.[7]

Friendship is based on having some interest in common. For someone pursuing the spiritual path, the most natural basis for friendship would be a shared desire to walk that path. If love should happen to grow out of such a friendship, so be it, but let love develop in its own way and in its own time.

Ella Wheeler Wilcox writes:

> All love that has not friendship for its base,
> Is like a mansion built upon the sand.[8]

In the Song of Solomon, Solomon's bride says:

> Do not arouse or awaken love
> until it so desires.[9]

Keeping It Real

Lucille Yaney, a therapist and good friend, has developed quite an understanding of relationships in her work with clients over many years. The advice she gives to her clients is that the primary characteristic to look for in a prospective partner is someone who is "normal." By this she means someone you can relate to in a natural and comfortable way.

To look for somebody who is normal might sound uninteresting or obvious, but her point is that people often don't find out who someone really is until they are well into a relationship. It is also a matter of whether you want to have a peaceful partnership or you want to have the competition, one-upmanship and drama that goes on in many marriages.

People will come to Lucy when they are in the midst of these marriages, and they will say that it came as a complete surprise when they found out what this person they married was really like. But after talking with them for a while, she usually finds out that all the signs were there in the very first date or meeting. The person just did not know what to look for.

When you date someone for the first time and you come away from the meeting feeling comfortable, that is usually a good sign. If you feel that you have gotten to know the person, if you feel real and they feel real and the flow is there, then generally the main core of the relationship is on solid footing and it has the potential to work. If you were able to be real and able to be comfortable around them, even in that very early stage of the relationship, then there is likely to be peace in the relationship if it develops.

Be wary if you feel incredible passion and excitement early on. If there are fireworks in the early stages of a relationship, if you feel swept off your feet, if there is flattery and lots of drama, this is often a warning sign of later problems. The drama is generally an exaggeration and a sign that the other person is distancing themselves from their true self. Beware also if you find that you cannot be yourself or if you feel as if you are starting to distance yourself from your true self.

If you feel swept off your feet at the beginning of a relationship, if there is lots of drama, this is often a warning sign of later problems.

The highest energy you feel, the most alive, is when you have a strong connection with your higher self. This is your ultimate source of energy. When you are under your own I AM Presence and Christ Self, you feel real. You care for yourself and have self-respect. But when you start to veer away from that connection, you start to feel unreal, and then you begin to act that way. You start to do what other people want you to do rather than what you need to do. When you do this, you will have a drop in your energy. There is a subtle depression that descends when you start to pretend to be something that you are not or try to be what someone else wants you to be. Your self-support diminishes and your self-respect also takes a dive.

One way to compensate for this drop in energy is to engage your emotional body. Rather than using your spiritual self for energy, you can use your emotional body to hype yourself up. That is where the drama comes into the relationship.

If you lose your self-respect, the other tendency is to think that the other person is the greatest catch in the world. Why? Because he or she is now going to compensate for what you lack. This person will make up for all for your unrealness and provide the support that you need. There is a tendency to exaggerate good aspects, and in only seeing the good and ignoring the faults, to become idolatrous of the other person. And if he or she has a low level of self-esteem that matches your own, then that one may well accept the idolatry that you offer and step up onto the pedestal that you have created.

This can all seem to go well for a while, especially if there is no real commitment and in the excitement of the dating scene. But if you want to deepen the relationship or if you get married, after a while it no longer works. The other person doesn't fulfill your expectations and give you everything you want—and how could they? They fall off the pedestal and then each of you gets into resentment. Your emotional bodies take over and the drama escalates. The honeymoon is now well and truly over. And the marriage or relationship will probably not last much longer because we just can't keep up that kind of pretense at close quarters for a long time.

These kinds of relationships could be karmic in nature. A psychologist might say you have matched your unreal selves. The unreal self of each of you balances the unreal self of the other. In fact it was your unreal selves or your incomplete selves that provided the attraction in the first place. And when Lucy works with clients in this situation, they usually find that it was all there at that first meeting.

Even though drama is a warning sign of a karmic relationship, some people definitely like drama and they may have things to learn from such relationships. On the positive side, the drama can push you to resolve things. You can definitely grow in a drama-filled relationship. And you will hear people saying, "I have grown and changed and he or she has forced me to be a better person."

If you want your marriage to be a non-stop process of change and initiation which is beyond the normal, then yes, you can get into this kind of marriage or relationship and learn from it. But this is very difficult to live with day after day. It can end up feeling like a twenty-four hour a day therapy session, and there are better places to do that than to live with it in your own home. You can usually learn these lessons about yourself in dealings with family and coworkers or in other social situations.

Spiritually speaking, every relationship has a meaning. From a psychological perspective, the purpose of dating is to spend enough time with a person that you can really begin to see what's underneath. What is their intent? What is their true motivation?

That is why we need to develop discernment when we date. Listen to what the other person is saying and to their voice and how they say it. Be careful if the voice sounds affected or disconnected or does not feel real. Pay attention to how you feel when you are around them and how they make you feel. And be willing to see all this for what it is—rather than what you would like it to be—and to be true to your own Real Self.

Commitment and Intimacy

Many people who see the problems with the current routines of dating have decided to abandon dating altogether—or at least call it something different. Some like to use the word *courtship*. It is a quaint term, one that reminds us of the values of a different era. More importantly, it conveys the sense that their pursuing a romantic relationship has a purpose.

There is a place for dating, whatever name is used for it. In order to know if they want to make a deeper commitment, two people usually need to spend time together, learn about one another, discuss what is important to them. The difference is that there is a greater purpose than just enjoying dating for its own sake.

In this kind of dating there are clear expectations. This doesn't mean a commitment that marriage will be the end point. It is not a pre-engagement. There is no promise of an ongoing relationship. There is a commitment to honor the other person and not play games—not to encourage love or commitment from another person without being open to the possibility of responding in kind.

Some people argue that there is nothing wrong with going into a relationship of limited commitment as long as both parties are aware of this from the outset. What if they are both just looking for fun and nothing more? It all depends on what you are looking for from life. Many people do live like this, and many people will tell you after years that it is not fulfilling.

Along with commitment, a healthy approach to dating also encourages respect for both physical and emotional intimacy. This point of view is almost revolutionary today, given that intimacy without commitment seems to have become the norm in popular culture.

One group of people swimming against this tide are conservative Christians. However, their advocacy of celibacy before marriage is often based on following the rules of scripture rather than a deeper understanding of spiritual principles. With this limited approach people can get stuck on the rules. Physical and technical virginity becomes the goal, and people can fall into the trap of thinking that any level of physical or emotional intimacy short of actual sexual intercourse is acceptable.

The decision to pursue a relationship of the heart is a serious one for those who also seek to pursue a spiritual path. It is important to know what our goal is in life, and then to make choices that will lead us closer to that goal and not further away.

This often puts people in the very difficult situation of trying to stop before things go "too far." However, just before "too far" is the most difficult time to stop, since powerful emotional and physical energies are already aroused at that point. And even if things don't go too far physically, there is the price that is paid mentally, emotionally and spiritually for an intimacy that is shared too early and too often.

The decision to pursue a relationship of the heart is a serious one for those who also seek to pursue a spiritual path. We all have choices as to how we will spend the allotment of time and energy we receive in this embodiment, and we will all live with the consequences of those choices. It is important to know what our goal is in life, and then to make choices that will lead us closer to that goal and not further away.

Before deciding to enter into a romantic involvement with someone, there are some important things to think about. Is there a higher purpose for this relationship? Does it add or detract from your spiritual growth? Does it support your spiritual path?

If you are not ready to make a commitment to the other person, is it fair to pursue intimacy? Even if you think you may be able to walk away from the relationship, what if the other person can't so easily walk away from feelings once awakened? Is it fair to start the ball rolling if you know that you plan to bail out and leave the other person hanging?

How much of yourself will you give to the other person before a commitment has been made? How much will you let the other person into your own life emotionally and physically?

Decide what your boundaries will be and plan your activities so as to stay within them. If you find things are getting more intense or moving faster than you are ready for, take a step back and reset your boundaries. Perhaps spend less time together or spend your time together in group settings, rather than alone.

Watch for signs that there is a problem. Are you starting to obsess about the relationship or think about the other person all the time? Is the relationship interfering with important goals in your spiritual life or mission? Is it causing you to isolate yourself from other important relationships in your life?

If you see these signs or have other concerns, take a step

back and focus on your spiritual work. Remember that emotional intensity isn't a reliable sign that this is the right person for you. The real guide is a quiet, inner knowing, and the intensity of emotions can make it more difficult to attune to that voice.

Consciously place all of the emotional energy around the relationship, and the relationship itself, in the violet flame. Call for clear vision of the way forward. And if you have concerns about the relationship, it may be helpful to talk through them with an older mentor or trusted advisor—in preference to the other person in the relationship. A mentor can give you feedback and share an independent perspective, separate from the strong emotions that can make clear thinking more challenging.

If in the course of pursuing the relationship you find that this is not the right person for you, it is best to call an end to it sooner rather than later. Don't let the other person think there is something there when there is not. That is not kind to either of you.

Setting Boundaries

Physical and emotional intimacy are closely connected, and if you are pursuing a romantic relationship with someone, it is important for each of you to think about what level of intimacy you can be comfortable with. As love grows and emotional intimacy naturally increases, it becomes even more important to have a clear idea of what your physical boundaries will be. How close can you be physically before you start to have a build-up of energy in the lower chakras that becomes a burden to one or the other or both?

It is a fact of human nature that physical contact can begin the flow of energy in a spiral that ultimately moves toward sexual fulfillment. And once that spiral has begun, it is difficult to reverse the flow of energy. So if you have decided that you are not going to engage in sexual intercourse before you are married, you have to decide where intercourse begins. And you need to decide ahead of time, because the situation can quickly get out of control.

If you have not set good boundaries, you may find that the energies of your chakras begin to descend, but they do not rise again, precisely because intercourse does not take place. Then the energies are stuck in the lower chakras.

Over time, unless the energy is being raised, there is a build-up of energy that requires more interaction for its fulfillment. At first, hand-holding may be satisfying. Then this is not enough, and the relationship progresses to kissing and more physical contact. Then the physical side of the relationship moves to another level.

This is even more likely to happen if you have been sexually active in the past, since your energies are accustomed to flowing in those channels. Unless you have developed self-mastery, it requires relatively little stimulus for you to require the full experience of sexual intercourse to find peace again or release. Your body has been trained to respond in that way.

You may decide, therefore, that you want to ease off the physical contact and emphasize other aspects of the relationship when you are getting to know one another or when you are engaged. Place an emphasis instead on outdoor and other physical activities, involvement with other people, conversations and sharing, prayer and service together.

For women, it is also important to consider what you wear. Most women have no idea how big a part visual stimulus plays in generating sexual energy in men, and an outfit that they think of as attractive may unwittingly be the cause of a struggle.

Don't buy into all the trends of modern fashion where the criterion for looking good is often to be sexually alluring. A good starting point might be to ask the question, "What would my father think of me wearing this on a date?" You could also ask your boyfriend for an honest opinion, and be willing to listen if he suggests that a favorite outfit might be traded in for something a little less revealing. Be kind to one another and do not be the cause of another's temptation.

Here are the stories of two couples and how they handled this phase of their relationship.

Sally and Jason were both in their forties and had been in a relationship for about a year. Neither had been married before, but Sally had been sexually active some years earlier. Now she had decided that she wanted to remain celibate until she found the right person, and she really thought that Jason was the one. Jason had not been sexually active before and was somewhat shy.

Jason wanted to sleep with Sally, but she was staying true to her commitment and did not get involved physically. She was, however, finding it increasingly difficult to cope with the energies that were arising when they were together.

Jason was reluctant to commit to marriage, having never been married before and having seen the devastation his parents' marriage and divorce caused. He said he loved Sally and he could not imagine his life without her, but he was nervous.

Sally decided to give Jason a timeline. She let him know that within two months she needed to know either that he would marry her or let her go. In the meantime, they monitored their time together. They pursued outdoor activities that got them active physically and did not allow their energies to stagnate in the lower chakras. No more late night cuddles by the fire. A quick kiss goodnight was fine.

"It is the only way right now," said Sally. "I could not take it anymore. I love Jason, but he is just going to have to decide—and soon." If not, she would be moving on.

Jason did ask Sally to marry him. They are very happy in their life together and they discovered that they are truly compatible—emotionally, sexually and in every way.

When Gena and Andres first met, they were in their early twenties. They both knew that this was it. Both had been sexually active some years earlier, but now they wanted their love to be pure and perfect until they married. They decided together on some strict guidelines for their behavior, and they kept one another in check. No long kisses. Some hand holding was OK. They decided on a short engagement before their marriage.

Gena says it was definitely the right way for them. They were very happy on their wedding day, and they share a deep and abiding love.

Engaged couples can embrace and love one another in a way that contributes to their expression of love but does not go beyond the level where the embracing builds a momentum of sexual energy that becomes uncomfortable for either partner. Often it is the prolongation of physical contact that produces the problems of over-stimulation. It is up to the couple to draw the line where they know that it has to be drawn for them.

To a greater or lesser extent, we all feel the energies of the world pulling us from time to time. The lowering of energies in the body, often through the mesmerism of sexual fantasy, takes our minds away from the *now*. It prevents us from concentrating on those things that we could be doing to further our situation in life, whether through education, work or service.

As soon as we feel the downward pull, it is up to us to draw a boundary, pull back our energy and raise the energy to the upper chakras. When you can do this, you will have a greater sense of freedom and an ability to make enlightened choices.

Engagement

When they are engaged, many couples arrange dates that are great fun or very romantic. This is wonderful from time to time, but it is also important to do normal, everyday things together. Observe how each of you behaves under the stresses of everyday life. See one another in all kinds of real-life circumstances so that there are no surprises or rude awakenings if you do decide to marry.

It is also a time to think about meeting one another's families, if this has not already happened. For teenagers, parents should know about relationships and be involved from the very beginning. But for adults in relationships, it can be a two-edged sword to have a potential partner become too involved with family at an early stage. If he or she has an accepted place at the family dinner table, it becomes more difficult to end the relationship, even if it becomes clear that it has no future.

There may also be pressure from family members that makes it more difficult to attune to the inner voice: "He seems such a nice young man. When are you two going to get married?"

On the other hand, parents can often bring perspective and wisdom from their years of experience. It may be very helpful to talk things over with them to clarify your own thoughts and feelings about the relationship. A minister or other trusted mentor may also play a similar role.

One thing to be aware of when you are engaged or in a serious relationship with another person is the false concept that a couple need to have sexual relations before marriage to see if they are sexually suited. This idea is based on an unrealistic and limited concept of sex as a physical experience.

Popular thought tells us that we do not need to be in love to have great sex. The focus on sex is often physical sensations. There are hundreds of books, DVDs and courses with techniques to have "great sex," but at a soul level this does not satisfy the deep need that we have to be loved. When the chakras are purified and the electronic belt is cleared, the natural flow of energies between man and woman is just that—natural.

If you really love one another and the person is the right one, then generally everything else at other levels will also work out. All of the four lower bodies will mesh properly and the sexual relationship will be fine.

Engagement is a time for spiritual work in preparation for marriage. It is an opportunity for a couple to work on transmuting records of karma between them through the use of the violet flame. This sets the stage for the best possible start to marriage.

Couples who decided to wait until they were married to become physically intimate often say that they are very happy with their decision. They felt that it was worth the wait and that this path allowed them to bring a greater purity and light to their marriage. They knew that their love and intimacy was deeper than just the sexual experience. They also knew that they had a certain mastery of their energies that would serve them well if they might need to be apart at times during marriage.

Therapist Sue Patton Thoele puts it well: "Don't marry

unless you are passionately in love but wait until you are married to express your passion."[10] Couples who desire to save the fruition of their love for marriage will agree together that they will keep their energies in check. They avoid situations where they might be tempted beyond what they will be able to deal with.

The time of engagement is also a time for spiritual work in preparation for marriage. It is an opportunity for a couple to work on transmuting records of karma between them through the use of the violet flame. This sets the stage for the best possible start to a marriage.

For most people, this karma includes a residue of negative substance in their lower chakras, whether from this life or as records and momentums from past lives. When they marry, they can transmute this with the violet flame. If it can be cleared before marriage, all the better. This will start the marriage on a higher plane, free of previous negative momentums and patterns of other relationships.

Most importantly, when you are getting to know someone or you are engaged, before you move to make a deeper commitment, you want to know that it is the right step, with the right person, at the right time. The more that can be cleared spiritually, the easier it will be to know this.

Expectations in Marriage

Every marriage is a contract of love. We take our vows before the altar, a formal commitment that we make to one another and to God, but our agreement also extends to many other levels, and we each have needs and expectations that we hope will be met in a marriage.

Sometimes people walk into marriage with preconceived notions as to how it is supposed to be, but they have not spoken with their future partner about these expectations. It is far better to talk these things over together before the marriage. Loving discussion about your desires and what is important to each of you sets a foundation for open communication throughout your married life.

Sit down together and share. What do you each expect out of marriage? What are your needs, your hopes, your dreams, your spiritual aspirations? What do you want and expect from one another?

It is helpful to remember that men and women often have different needs. A woman needs a man to be able to listen to her, to spend time with her, show love and appreciation through loving words and tender touching that is not always sexual. Does he realize that when she does things for him, she is showing her love for him?

Similarly a man needs a woman to be able to love, respect

and nurture him and to make their home a safe haven for him. Does she realize that he naturally expresses the depth of his love in the sexual relationship and that he often thrives on his profession and his work?

Discuss and agree on important issues before you exchange your marriage vows. What are your expectations for privacy and independence? What are your expectations around levels of sexual activity? What are your values around money, debt, spending and saving? Where would you like to live? How do you feel about issues relating to children and child raising?

Another thing to consider is whether this person is a part of your soul group, the mandala of people with whom you are meant to be. There are also young souls and there are older souls. Young souls don't have the same length of history or the depth of experience that an older soul has. So if you are an older soul and you enter a relationship with a younger soul, you may feel that lack of depth and inner connection. You may feel that something is missing in the relationship.

There may be nothing wrong with the other soul other than they are a younger soul and therefore not capable of the same depth of relationship at this stage in their soul evolution. Give them a few more incarnations and they may develop that depth and richness that comes with experience.

Generally people are happier for the long run if they are with their same soul grouping and those of similar soul evolution. This is another aspect of being "equally yoked."

Ask yourself if there is something that you can't live with in this person. If your answer is yes, this requires thought and prayer. Sometimes people get married with the idea that they will change the other person after the marriage—but this usually doesn't work, and it isn't really fair. You can't change the rules after you have tied the knot.

If you feel that this is the right relationship for you, and yet there is something about the other person you feel you can't live with, there are two options.

The first is to take another look at yourself. Is this really something you can't live with? Can you change yourself or learn to live with it? Or can you tolerate it given the fact that there is a greater love that binds you?

It is important to be realistic. Don't just hope that love will some-how work it out. Love may work it out. But it is better if you can work it out before the marriage so that you will really know that you can do it.

> *The hallmark of true love is liberty, not the suppression of our true self for or by another.*

The second option is to try to change the other person. Of course, this is not really possible unless the other person wants to change. And if you do choose this option, the fair way to do it is to postpone the marriage and try to change the person beforehand!

Whichever option you choose, the violet flame can help. Sometimes the things we feel we can't live with in another person are karmic patterns or personality traits that trigger our own. We get irritated when we see something in another that we don't like in ourselves. We push each other's buttons because we have buttons to be pushed, unresolved issues in our own subconscious.

The violet flame can smooth the rough edges of personality and karma that grate on us. After three or six months of violet flame, you may find that things you thought you could not live with are no longer a problem. Perhaps the violet flame changed the other person. Perhaps it changed your reaction. Perhaps it changed both of you.

It is also possible that after using the violet flame you may find a confirmation that you can't live with this thing in the other person and the relationship is not right for you. This may also be a very good outcome.

Remember the advice of Saint Paul—"Be not unequally yoked together ... for what communion hath light with darkness?"[11] The hallmark of true love is liberty, not the suppression of our true self for or by another.

To Marry or Not

Whether or not to marry is a personal and private decision. Although God may bless a marriage, the relationship must also be hallowed and sanctified by the parties involved. Therefore, it remains for the couple to decide.

If you want a marriage to work, you should look for confirmation from within. Keep in mind that you will bear one another's karma, and only being deeply in love enables you to take on that burden.

If you are walking a spiritual path and see marriage as part of that path, you would do well to ask two questions when you are trying to decide whether or not to enter into a marriage.

The first question is this:

Have you considered whether your individual service will be enhanced, will be enriched and will be greater in the marriage union than it would be separately?

When your marriage is part of your spiritual journey, one plus one does not equal two. One plus one equals three, because there is you and your wife, or you and your husband, and the Holy Spirit between you. It is when the Holy Spirit is upon the altar of the marriage—whether in church or in the home or in the bedroom—that the marriage is valid in the eyes of God, for every phase of marriage should be sacred.

When you have this relationship in a marriage, each partner brings individual strengths to the relationship and these become complementary. Greater things are possible because you support one another and the Holy Spirit enters in to support you both.

Bringing forth children is one gift that you can give to one another and to the world when you are together, but this is only one of the blessings that the Holy Spirit may bestow through a marriage that is consecrated to a higher service.

The second question is this:

Are you deeply in love? Do you really have that deep fire burning in the heart, that fire that can commemorate your love for God?[12]

If you don't have that love, the marriage will not withstand the onslaughts of the world. It will never be the whirling fire that is able to overcome every adversity.

A successful marriage on the spiritual path has these two requirements: the greater service to God, greater than you can render alone, and an intense, fiery love.

People sometimes want to get married because they think it's the thing to do and they want to have children, but they really haven't experienced that greater love nor do they have any conception of how they, together, can make that one-plus-one equal three in service. Sometimes these marriages do endure, as karma and circumstance provide the impetus to growth for each soul and they discover a greater and deeper love that is born in the crucible of experience. But without a higher commitment, many people enter into marriage unprepared for the challenges it faces today.

The true ideal of marriage is not to expect but to give. A

successful marriage is constant giving. You enter a marriage and immediately you say, "What can I give? What can I do for my spouse? What can I do for the children?"

A focus on giving rather than receiving should be at the center of all our relationships, even our relationship with God. We go to God to love him. The love that returns should be secondary, otherwise our relationship to God may become a selfish one. Sometimes people meditate on God simply so they can feel the bliss of his light descending on them. This is not the true purpose of meditation. The highest aim of meditation is to give love to God. The purpose of marriage should be the same.

Marriage should not dominate the spiritual path. It should be a sacred and highly attuned and disciplined instrument of the path of initiation. It is not to be entered into lightly, because it is a more intense initiation than the individual path. It is more intense because it always includes two—two sets of chakras, two causal bodies, two electronic belts. And if there is not true harmony and unity of purpose, instead of becoming a polarity where one plus one equals three, the two can become an opposition, where one minus one equals zero.

Marriage should not dominate the spiritual path. It should be a sacred and highly attuned and disciplined instrument of the path of initiation.

Ultimately, we need to transcend the sense of duality in marriage. Instead of thinking of ourselves as two separate people, we can think of ourselves as one—because the Father-Mother God is one. All our troubles come when we're two people with two selfish sets of interests. This does not mean that we cannot have separate interests or careers or friends. It does not mean that we lose our individuality, but we examine things through the filter of "us" and "ours" rather than "me" and "mine."

We should not enter marriage thinking of it as a brother-sister relationship or a substitute for a family relationship that we did not experience in childhood. Rather, marriage is based on the profound oneness of being in love.

One wife-to-be once told her spiritual teacher, "I think we have work to do together." The teacher said, "That's fine, but the reason to marry is that you are madly in love."

Both are key ingredients for a successful marriage on the spiritual path.

6
Marriage
and the
Spiritual Path

There is no relationship in this world this side of heaven that can be sustained merely by romantic love and its union. A relationship is sustained by hard work and striving, giving of the self and expecting nothing in return.

Expect nothing and you will never be disappointed. Be the giver and find how soon you receive the gift of love in return.

CHAMUEL AND CHARITY
ARCHANGELS OF LOVE

Marriage as an Initiation on the Path

While customs around marriage have changed in many ways, the institution of marriage has endured throughout the history of humanity. Marriage mirrors a spiritual reality that is present in everyone's inner awareness—the eternal union with one's twin flame.

Despite what popular culture might portray, no relationship of enduring worth can be built primarily on a foundation of sexual experiences or physical pleasure. Marriage on the spiritual path is intended to be far more than this. It is an experience of the union of two souls, and this union may occur at the level of any of the chakras. The bliss of that divine union may be an entirely different experience from what the world might contemplate in marriage.

We need to beware of accepting the world's concepts of marriage and the fulfillment we should find there, because this can only lead to disappointment. We cannot expect that a mere physical relationship could meet the need of the soul to rise to ever higher levels of consciousness.

Elizabeth Clare Prophet provides a unique perspective on the opportunities marriage offers for spiritual growth:

We must not take the world's concept of marriage and put so many demands upon marriage, expecting it to be the answer to all of our problems. Sometimes people have unrealistic hopes that in marriage somehow all the pain, the sorrow, the problems of life will be eliminated and all of our greatest longings, including fantasies and subconscious motivations, will be fulfilled and all our dreams will come true.

This is one of the illusions that society portrays for us and thereby encourages us to put many demands and strains upon our marriage and our marriage partner. The wife expects all of these things to be fulfilled by the husband. The husband expects all of these things to be fulfilled by the wife. And the gods themselves could not possibly fulfill all the expectations and preconceived ideas that we have of the supreme bliss of the married state. Marriages are stretched to the breaking point because partners are demanding what marriage is not intended to give.

We need to give some definition to marriage, what it is capable of giving to us and what we are capable of giving to it. We should have a healthy, practical, down-to-earth awareness of what must take place in marriage, and then we can decide whether we will strive for a marriage that is simply the human custom of husband and wife or a marriage that has the goal of the soul and the spirit being one.

Both of these are valid marriages on earth, but society teaches us only the one. It teaches us the marriage between partners, between husband and wife. But the world says very little about the marriage that is an initiation on the path of life, that is the means for experiencing the spiritual marriage that can exist between the soul and God in a very real, tangible and fulfilling relationship.

The only way a marriage can work on the spiritual path is for husband and wife to understand that marriage must contain the totality of God—the totality of human relationships as well as divine relationships.

Roles in marriage should not be rigid. The wife bears the role of wife, but she may also fulfill every other aspect of the feminine nature of God at some time or another. At times she may be mother or daughter or sister. She may be child or she may be the mature matriarch, the patroness of life. At the same time, the husband should not expect to rigidly play the role of husband. God does not do this. God appears to us as Father, as Son, as Holy Spirit, as brother, neighbor, friend, as partner on the way.

All of these relationships, including the relationship of monk and nun or priest and priestess, can be fulfilled within marriage, and these relationships change from moment to moment. If we are always demanding of our spouse the epitome of our concept of what husband or wife should be, we are going to be sadly disappointed, because no one is strictly one role or one person.

Marriage is the movement of the cloven tongues of fire. And when you observe physical fire, you see that you can never capture the flame and say, "This is the shape of the flame." A flame never has a fixed shape—it keeps moving. And so do these twin flames of the Holy Spirit which the marriage commemorates. These flames in the marriage are constantly leaping, moving, and taking on different characteristics of God.

If marriage partners are two flames, they ought to be blending in harmony, and when one takes one shape, the other molds itself around that shape. This is the day-to-day creativity and flow of the love that ought to exist between husband and wife and between the soul and the I AM Presence. But if we try to make our relationship fit the rigid mold of what we see in civilization today and what society tells us should be in marriage, we will lose out on the richness and the depth that God has given us to experience.[1]

We look at life with the understanding that whoever we are dealing with is God. The person is God—in manifestation. The divine flame is God. The potential is God. And we must love that person with our whole heart, with the purest and highest love that we would have for God and for our twin flame. That love is liberating. It is a transmutative force.

We need forgiveness in relationships. We need liberally to forgive others and to forgive ourselves, because that's the whole point of karma. We all have much to forgive and much to be forgiven for, or we would not find ourselves on this planet at this point in time and space.

So it doesn't matter if you're married to your twin flame or if you've ever met your twin flame. What matters is that you realize the sacredness of marriage and the relationship of man and woman, and that this polarity is always representative of "Alpha and Omega"—the Masculine/Feminine Co-Creators of Life in the white-fire body of the Godhead depicted by the Chinese as the T'ai Chi.[2]

The ancient prophets spoke of their experiences in seven heavens, levels of the etheric octave where they journeyed out of the body. As we work to spiritualize our consciousness, we can also have these experiences as our souls leave the body in sleep each night and we journey to the etheric retreats of the ascended masters. Couples may journey to the retreats together and have truly transcendent experiences there, returning to start the new day with a common awareness of cosmic consciousness that far transcends the world's understanding of relationships.

Working through Karma

The understanding that relationships and marriage have a higher goal gives a new vision of what the joys and bliss of marriage can be. But along with this there is also the necessity of working through karma.

Most people don't know what they're getting when they get married. They don't understand that they have made a vow to share one another's karma. They want the joys of marriage but not the responsibilities. But then they wake up one morning and find that "the honeymoon is over."

In the early stages of a relationship, we tend to see everything that is good and beautiful and wonderful about the other person—the light of the causal body. All of this is shared in marriage. But once the marriage vows have been taken, the burden of the electronic belt is also shared. The love and light of the causal body is meant to be what enables the couple to overcome their negative momentums and balance their karma.

Marriage is calculated to bring out the best and the worst in both partners, and you can be sure that it will. The worst is brought to the surface so that it can be faced and overcome. And sometimes the best that is latent within us only comes to the fore when we are faced with the challenges of life.

Along with spiritual work, a practical key for working through the karmic issues in marriage is being able to talk with one another about issues as they come. When your partner does something that irritates you or pushes your buttons, this is a sign of karma coming up.

You may wonder, "Doesn't he (or she) understand how I feel?" Quite possibly not, unless you say something. Sometimes there is a tendency to think, even subconsciously, "If he really loved me, he would know what I want without me having to tell him." But it's really not fair to expect your spouse to be a mind-reader.

Marriage is not easy. Marriage is work. And our most important work is the work of God that we can accomplish through marriage. Jesus said, "The Father worketh hitherto, and I work,"[3] and this is what we are all called to do. When each one in the marriage partnership is dedicated to God's work, then the marriage works because it's unselfish. You join hands to do a job for God and that job is what is important.

Sometimes the work is very practical, as in the raising of children. Sometimes it is a joint service in a larger sphere—your community, your nation, or the world. Whatever your calling to service, when there is the vision of a higher goal, the pettiness of little arguments and disagreements flies to the wind. There is a job to be done.

As one happily married couple put it, "When we look at our marriage as the work of the Lord and remember how much we love each other, everything comes together."

Putting God First

arriage is a means of learning about oneself and one another. The husband is the teacher of the wife and the wife is the teacher of the husband. In the relationship of twin flames, the Holy Christ Self of the twin flame is always your teacher.

Through marriage, as each internalizes the positive qualities of the other, each can become the androgynous whole. When they stand apart as separate individuals, each one can then contain the wholeness of the other and be that complete whole. When they have achieved this, even if there is a sudden separation or parting or death, each one remains the Divine Whole. In this way love can triumph over death.

The perversion of this love is possessiveness and dependence. This is one reason for the failure of marriage. If you are totally dependent on your mate for your own wholeness and for your own realization of God, then the relationship may become a hindrance to spiritual progress instead of a help. In such a case, you may find that God will separate you from that mate, even if just for a time.

I had this experience early in my own marriage. One day Mrs. Prophet said to me, "Are you more attached to your husband than to God? Because if you are, God will take him from you." I very quickly said, "Oh, no, no, no." But deep down, I knew it was true.

It wasn't too much later that I found myself on several road trips for six weeks at a time. I had waited so long to find Peter, and I couldn't bear the thought of being apart from him. So it was a very difficult test to be separated like that. While I was away we would talk when I could find a pay phone (this was in the days before cellphones), but I would count the days before I would return.

I remembered what Mrs. Prophet had said. The message was burned within me as to what my priorities needed to be. I learned that even though we were separated for a time, we would be together again. I came to find peace in being apart. And I have learned that I can be alone and be OK, because I am never apart from God.

The higher way of marriage is for husband and wife to recognize and revere the divine in one another. The wife bows to the light of the Christ within her husband, and the husband reveres the Divine Mother in his wife. This does not mean that the wife bows to his human creation or that he reveres her human creation.

In every marriage, the husband and wife should put God first rather than one another. After all, God is the one who has brought us together to glorify him. Therefore, no matter what tests may come to either party in the marriage, we cannot allow our spouse to separate us from our relationship with God.

There are always moments on the path of life when the husband or the wife must pass through a spiritual test. The nature of these tests is that the gate is narrow and only one can pass through at a time. Then the husband or wife must be released to walk through that gate of initiation alone.

While that is happening, your love for God and for the soul has to be so great that you don't seek to deprive your mate of the opportunity of a test, even if it is hard to see them going through a great trial. Nor do you try to hold them back to maintain a human comfortability in the relationship in a situation where that one is seeking to change and go higher in consciousness. At these times you pray, offer support, and love your spouse, but allow that one the space they need to pass the tests of life.

Sometimes the spouse does not pass through the gate and a test is failed. This may take many forms. Most devastating are those tests failed through the dregs of drugs or alcoholism, repeated unfaithfulness, or many forms of abuse that simply are intolerable to the God within you. This is one of life's most painful experiences.

You may reach a point where your higher love for God means that you will say, "If necessary, I will stand alone. I will not follow my spouse on a path of self-destruction, because if I go down that path, there is no hope for either of us to return. I will keep the flame and I will wait for the day when my spouse once again desires to walk the path of light."

This is the greatest of all tests in a marriage, where we must decide that no outer relationship can stand between us and our relationship with God. This may necessitate periods of separation—or even ultimately of divorce. But if we do not stand firm in this test, we lend our own light to reinforce the choice of a path of self-destruction.

If we feel that our relationship to God is threatened and may be destroyed by discord, then we must make a decision to protect that aspect of the flame that is ours to keep. It is important to give love and support as a means to solve the problems within marriage. But if you have to give that love and support over and over again to the extent that you are compromising your own reason for being and your purpose in life and draining your own life-blood in the process, you may reach the point where you have to decide whether this marriage can work in harmony or whether it can't. Only you can know what the answer is for you and your marriage.

A marriage depends on what each side of the marriage contract decides that they are able to give. If one gives too much, one has nothing left of oneself. This becomes a false sacrifice whereby you may lose your own self-mastery, your integrity and your spirituality.

On the other hand, we must be careful that we do not fall into selfishness, a holier-than-thou attitude or a sense of aloofness. This in itself can be due to a lack of spiritual attainment, whereby people decide that they are too good for someone else and use this as a justification for withholding love and the legitimate gift of self in support of another.

In all of these decisions, the great need is for balance, neither too far to the left nor the right, but always centered in the Middle Way of the Buddha. In this way, marriage can fulfill its highest purpose.

Kahlil Gibran spoke of this in *The Prophet*:

> Give your hearts, but not into each other's keeping.
> For only the hand of Life can contain your hearts.
> And stand together, yet not too near together:
> For the pillars of the temple stand apart,
> And the oak tree and the cypress grow not
> in each other's shadow.[3]

The Ritual of the Archangels

C harity, the feminine archangel of the ray of love, has given a ritual and a meditation for the sealing of the sacred circle of love within the marriage union:

O my children, let your love be the commemoration of the fusion of the cloven tongues of the Spirit. Now then, take the ritual which the archangels practice at the rising and the setting of the sun when the torch of love is passed by angels of the dawn and angels of the dusk. Take the ritual of the archangels and make it all your own, and prove thereby the victory of love on Terra. Prove that your love is the holy habitation of the LORD God of hosts and that this love, by your will firmed in the fire of God-determination, will not be defiled by the hordes of the night.

Stand together facing the chart of the I AM Presence and make your inner attunement with the star of your divinity. Meditate upon your heart and the flame therein and behold the arc ascend into the center of the Divine Monad. Now take your right hand and dip it into the fires of your heart and draw the circle of our oneness around yourselves as you stand in adoration of the One. Visualize this circle, twelve feet in diameter, as a line of sacred fire. It is your ring-pass-not. Within that circle of oneness is the forcefield of Alpha and Omega; and you focus the T'ai chi, the plus and minus of cosmic energies, where you are.

Let the flow of your love be not in imitation of the idolatrous generation. Let it not be the mechanization of sex as the Luciferians have popularized their sordid and sadistic ways. The flow of the Holy Spirit twixt father and mother is for the birth of the Divine Manchild, first within each heart and then in the Bethlehem babe. Seek not the thrills of sensuality or the titillation of mind or body, but seek the bliss of mutual reunion in the Presence.

Let your love be the reenactment of the alchemical marriage. Let your love be consecrated for the soul's ultimate reunion with the I AM Presence. So is the marriage ritual intended to be the rehearsal for the great drama of your soul's assumption into the flame of love for the rolling-up of the scroll of identity into the Great Silence of your own I AM THAT I AM and for the fusion of those twin flames of the Godhead when the I AM Presence of each half of the Divine Whole merges in the hallowed circle of God.

Seek the bliss of the raising of the Mother light—of *sushumna*, *ida* and *pingala*—as these form the caduceus energies that reveal your real identity in Christ. Let your bliss transcend the earthly senses, and let your light flow from all of the chakras to reinforce the divine polarity of the Father-Mother God in every level of consciousness to be outpictured in the seven major chakras and the five chakras of the secret rays.

Your marriage is made in heaven and you are wed to God. Daughters of the flame: Behold, thy Maker is thine husband. So be, with Mary, the handmaid of the Lord. Sons of the flame: The golden band you wear is the halo of the Cosmic Virgin, the bride descending out of heaven to consummate your love on earth.

As above, so below, the cosmic flow of Father-Mother God is intended to be shared in the sanctuary of the Holy Family. And it is intended to be sealed with the blessing of the true ministers of the Logos and to be guarded by purity in the holy of holies. The ark of the covenant is also a matrix of the protection of twin flames joined together in holy matrimony for a life of service to God and man. And the covering cherubim must be invoked daily, for they are the guardians of love in the planes of Mater.

Understand, O wise ones pursuing the law of the Logos, that if the fallen ones can destroy love, they can destroy all. For love is the foundation and the fountain of life. Love is the essence of creation.[4]

7
When Marriage Doesn't Work

What therefore God hath joined together, let not man put asunder.

JESUS

"What God Hath Joined Together ..."

God created you and your twin flame out of the same white-fire body in the beginning, and the story in Genesis of Eve being formed out of the rib of Adam is an allegory to illustrate this mystical concept.[1]

No one in heaven or on earth can separate you from your twin flame. That's why Jesus said, "What therefore God hath joined together, let not man put asunder."[2] No matter what the circumstances of your life might be, no one can separate you from your twin flame since you are always one in the white-fire core of being.

Yet marriages are made on earth for various reasons, and these are not necessarily the marriage made in heaven. People by their own choice come before the altar to receive a blessing, but this union is not something of which it can be said, "What God hath joined together ..."

Therefore karmic marriages may come and go. They are for a purpose, and so long as the karma remains (unless there are alternative means for working it out) they are binding. If we find ourselves in such a relationship, we can make it a celebration on earth of our inner union with our twin flame. This is lawful.

What is not lawful is to treat such a relationship

half-heartedly or even resentfully. If we think, "This is a karmic marriage, so I'll just make the best of it until I find my twin flame," this will simply delay the resolution of karma.

We must make the very best of a situation and not give up on a marriage unless we are given a very clear indication that this is the will of God. (Of course, this does not mean it is necessary to allow abuse or harm to oneself or one's children. In such a situation, take the necessary steps to protect life, including your own.) If there are problems in a relationship, counseling for one or both parties may be very helpful.

Given all this, there are situations where divorce does become necessary. The angels and masters in heaven are not opposed to divorce in these cases. When two people have tried everything, where there is not harmony between them and they are making more karma together than they would if they were apart, this is a lawful reason to consider that a divorce should take place.

The Painful Facts of Divorce

I f marriage were a mere physical union, divorce, when it occurs, would not be so emotionally devastating. Divorce is the surgery of pulling apart two who have become one; and all the battles about who owns what and who gets the children really center around the excruciating process of redefining one's self apart from the other self.

If you are dealing with a situation of divorce, having explored counseling and all other alternatives, it is important to take the situation to the altar in prayer. Do your best to be as harmonious as possible. Treat your spouse as you would like to be treated. Over-communicate rather than under-communicate. Do so in a courteous and respectful way. Even if you feel the other party is at fault, at all costs try to avoid assigning or implying blame.

Spiritually, the most important element is to make your way through the process without making more karma. This is often a challenge in the midst of the emotional intensity of a separation. If possible, give extra violet flame at this time to transmute any residual karma and to dissolve patterns of emotional attachments.

Just as in the honeymoon phase of a relationship people tend to see only the good in their partner, in the separation you often see only the negatives. Don't be surprised if things that you did not see earlier or that were simply interesting quirks now become extremely irritating. Realize that the person was probably not as good as they seemed during the honeymoon nor as bad as they seem now, and use the violet flame to smooth the rough aspects of the relationship.

There are many decisions to be made that may have a lasting impact on your life, the life of your spouse, and the lives of any children you may have. Do your best to stay centered and attuned with your Higher Self. When important meetings are to take place, say a prayer for all participants to meet in the heaven world the night before to discuss what is to take place and to reach the highest resolution, and ask that this resolution be brought to their outer awareness during the meeting in the physical.

Take good care of yourself and your children. Ask the guardian angel of each member of the family, including your partner, to help everyone through this difficult time. It is important to find the time to keep your spiritual practices going.

Talk the situation through with a counselor or good friend. This can be extremely helpful in working through the emotional issues of a painful situation. Choose someone who is good at listening and supportive, preferably someone who can remain very centered even when talking about difficult issues. If you find that your friend starts to become resentful or angry with your spouse or encourages these emotions in you, then it would be better to find someone else to confide in.

Talk to God, talk to your friends, talk to your pillow—but above all, keep your cool when talking to your spouse and when participating in legal proceedings. Some people find it very helpful to invite a friend to accompany them and help them stay centered during meetings and legal procedures.

If you do find yourself in legal proceedings, make sure to get a good lawyer. Avoid those whose emphasis in divorce is winning, making the other party pay, or enforcing your rights. Look for those who emphasize mediation rather than litigation and a cooperative approach to arriving at a resolution that will meet the needs of all parties.

Remember, the aim should never be to win or to make the other party pay for what they did—no matter how bad their behavior might have been. The aim is the best possible upbringing for your children and to balance your karma with your former spouse. Sometimes the balancing of karma requires giving more than might seem "fair" in the eyes of others, who see only the relationship as it was in this lifetime. But it may well be worth paying a price so you can be totally free to move on both physically and spiritually. Pray for an inner sense of what is right and just, both materially and spiritually.

Divorce proceedings are always emotionally challenging, especially if you or your spouse becomes combative or adversarial. However, patience and a loving heart will help to carry you through even the most difficult circumstances. Ask your guardian angel to help you to be patient and kind. Keep going back to forgiveness, and make it a point to be compassionate to everyone concerned.

As with any time of change, there are great possibilities for spiritual growth in the midst of pain. There is a sorting process involved in any separation. Most importantly it occurs on mental, emotional and spiritual levels. Two lives, two auras have become entwined in a marriage, and the process of separation is like pulling out the threads of a cloth that you have woven together. How do I feel and think about things, separate from my spouse? What things do I like to do? Who am I as a separate person? If you work through these things successfully, you will be able to acknowledge and claim what you gained from the relationship, leaving the rest behind.

These internal struggles are often reflected in the physical aspects of the separation. Who will get the house, the car, the favorite piece of furniture, the dog? Sometimes the struggles over seemingly small things take on a huge significance if they come to symbolize subconsciously the inner struggles of separation.

Who will get the house, the car, the favorite piece of furniture, the dog? Sometimes the struggles over seemingly small things take on a huge significance if they come to symbolize subconsciously the inner struggles of separation.

Being able to talk through the emotional issues with a trusted friend or advisor can make it easier to deal with the physical aspects of separation and divorce. It can help you to work through the real issues and not get stuck on the outer symbols. Mediation is nearly always a better approach than litigation.

If there are children involved, this brings a whole new dimension. You may be divorcing a spouse, but if you have children you will both continue to be parents to those children for the rest of your lives. It is inevitable that you will have an ongoing relationship, and how well children handle a divorce depends very much on how well their parents handle it.

A child's relationships with father and mother are key to psychological and soul development. These relationships are archetypal in the psyche, and if the child does not have a healthy relationship with a human father or mother, this may carry over into the adult having difficulty forming a healthy relationship with God as Father or God as Mother and with other people. It is therefore important for each parent to allow children to have an ongoing loving relationship with both parents.

When speaking with your children, always speak favorably of your former spouse. You may have your difficulties and disagreements, but don't share these with your children. Speak the truth, but find something positive or hopeful to say whenever possible. If you cannot find anything good to say, better to say nothing than belittle or run down the parent of your children.

Sharon's former spouse was addicted to amphetamines, never paid child support that was legally due, and rarely turned up for any of the children's activities. But she learned to say, "Your father loves you very much." She said it with conviction because she knew it was true in the very depths of his soul, even though his addictions often prevented him from demonstrating this love in any tangible way.

Do whatever it takes to have a harmonious (or at least civil) relationship with your former spouse to the extent that is necessary to handle your responsibilities as a parent. You can't hire a lawyer every time you need to decide who will pick up the children after soccer practice, where they will spend Christmas, or when your teenager can start dating. The sooner you can learn to work things out cooperatively rather than confrontationally, the better it will be for everyone—especially the children.

If you and your former spouse can decide to go through the divorce while remaining friends, this is the best approach. And it is a conscious choice you can make. Think about the day when your child is married. Wouldn't you and your spouse both like to be there and enjoy the occasion? How would you relate to one another then? Why not start now?

Even before a divorce is settled, it is important to set your soul's sail for the future. If you have already defined your spiritual goals, they are a foundation; if not, this is a good time to prayerfully consider those goals. Take your circumstances and future to the altar and ask God, "What is my next step? What is your will for me?" As you incline your mind and heart to God and listen within, you are beginning to redefine yourself apart from your spouse.

Sometimes you may have an intuitive sense as to the path ahead. Sometimes you may receive a clear vision of your future. Sometimes you may see no further than the very next step. The important point is to go to God. He is your best friend and holy confidant, and his comfort will help you through, no matter how difficult your outer circumstances might be.

Day by day, as you talk things over with God, you can strengthen your awareness of who you are as a spiritual being, as the mother or father of your children, and as the unique person that you are in this life. You are in the process of reclaiming and expanding your sense of self, your higher values and your goals in life.

Know that God loves you, your former partner, and your children. He wants the best for all of you, but it is up to you to reclaim the person you really are and to get on with your life and your spiritual path. So make a list of your favorite things, write down your values and insights about yourself, give your children and yourself a lot of love and appreciation, get help as you need it, and muster the courage to move on.

Linda is the recently divorced mother of three children.

While going through a separation, she said, "You do what you have to do." She and her former husband make it a point to tell their children that mommy and daddy both love them very much. They sit together at soccer games, they have harmonious exchanges when they meet to deliver the children for sleepovers. and they have learned to bite their tongues when necessary.

Linda has excellent support from family and friends. But even with all of this, she says it is not easy and it is often painful. She keeps reminding herself, "It's about the children. They are what's important."

Before Remarrying

If you have recently gone through a divorce, it is a good idea to wait for a period of time before thinking about entering another relationship or remarrying. There are profound reasons for this.

If you conclude that your marriage did not work because it was not right for you, it is important to consider why you entered into it in the first place. Very often it is because of karma and your psychology.

It is a spiritual law that your circumstances are a result of your karma and your psychology. If you change your karma and change your psychology, you can change your circumstances. Conversely, if you do not transmute the karma and overcome the negative aspects of your psychology that attracted you to the wrong person, you stand a very good chance of attracting to yourself a person from the same mold as the one you just divorced.

It will likely be the same problems, the same negative patterns, but in a different body with a different name. For example, you might vow never to marry another alcoholic, but then find yourself attracted to a person with a gambling problem or some other addiction. Until your own inner patterns are changed, the magnet is still there. If you move to a new relationship too quickly, you will likely not have changed enough to marry someone who is related to a higher level of yourself, because you have not yet had time and space to move to that higher level.

Psychologists tell us that the time necessary to pass though the stages of grieving after the death of a loved one is about two years. This is about how long it takes to fully let go of old patterns, to go through the sorting process, and to find again who you are as a separate individual. Divorce is a voluntary separation, but the process is similar in some ways, and twenty-four months is an excellent goal to set before dating or thinking about another relationship.

You may find that well-meaning friends or family members will encourage you to get into another relationship quickly to help you get over the sense of loss and to fill the vacuum, or even to "get back on the horse that threw you." But take the time you need as a God-given

Take the time of being single as a God-given opportunity to grow through prayer, introspection, psychological work and your spiritual practice.

opportunity to grow through prayer, introspection, psychological work and your spiritual practice.

Mariana knows this lesson well. She is recently divorced after being married for ten years to a man who she loved deeply but who was never able to return her love. He was constantly critical of what she wore, what she did, and who she was. He continually withheld sexual relations from her and told her that she was not attractive to him. Over a period of time she came to realize that this marriage would never work. Her husband refused to receive any counseling and eventually agreed to a divorce.

Mariana says, "I feel that I am meant to marry and have children, but I know that I must wait and work on my own psychology so that I don't attract another husband who is just like my old one. I have issues that I can trace back to my childhood, and I want to spend time working on my own wholeness so I can attract someone who is also whole."

The period of time after a divorce is a like a cosmic interval. Reassess all aspects of your life and make those changes that you have always wanted to make but have never had the time to concentrate on. Work hard on resolving your personal psychology and use the violet flame liberally. It is the energy of change and transmutation, and it can help you make positive changes in your life.

You may not have planned to go through the challenges of divorce and separation. But if this does come your way, make the most of the opportunity to learn and grow.

8
Spiritual
Exercises

Perfect love is a sacred fire that begins in the heart.

ELIZABETH CLARE PROPHET

Raising the Light

While we seek perfect love and hope to magnetize it to us, we also have to realistically deal with the challenges and burdens that we face when living in physical bodies in the modern world. And even though we may understand that the body is a temple for the evolving spirit, we still may struggle to live our lives as if this were so.

We may find ourselves moved by lesser desires even when we aspire to a higher way. We may have developed habits that overwhelm us at times when we are living in a world that seems counter to the direction we want to go. We may find that we have doubts and fears. And if the third-eye chakra is not clear, the spiritual vision and clear perception that could help us make wise choices may be lacking. It is said that karma blinds.

Spiritual exercises can make the difference. They can be the anchor that helps us to pull away from old momentums and brings us to a new place in consciousness. We can use them to increase the light within to magnetize the love of our life. And we can use them to invoke the transformative energies that can balance the karma that separates us from the loving relationship that God may have waiting for us.

This section takes you through some simple yet powerful spiritual tools to transform your world. The energy of the base chakra will naturally and gradually rise as you use these spiritual techniques. You will not necessarily feel the energy rising, because it will happen gradually, day by day. But after a few months of daily practice, you may look back and realize how far you have come. You may well find a sense of peace and wholeness that you have not known before.

Before we begin, a word of caution about working with energies of the base-of-the-spine chakra. There are techniques taught by gurus from the East that claim to accelerate the raising of the Kundalini. However, these practices can be dangerous— as the energy rises, it can activate karmic records and negative momentums in the chakras.

There is a safe way to work with the energies of the chakras and to raise the light. Instead of focusing directly on the lower chakras and raising the Kundalini, we can meditate on the upper chakras, from the heart to the crown. When we intensify the light in those centers, they become magnets to naturally draw up the energy from the base.

This action is enhanced when we clear negative energies from all of the chakras using the violet flame. The use of the violet flame can be a very effective tool for clearing barriers to the raising of the light. It can also clear past records and habit patterns of lowering the light, making it easier to develop new and positive momentums.

When the chakras are cleared by the action of the violet flame, the energy rises of its own accord, and the heart and third eye are freed from blocks to our perception of what is real.

Meditation on the Chakras

Sending the violet flame into the chakras, visualizing the flame and meditating on the flame can be most effective. As you give these mantras, visualize the light of the violet flame rising through each chakra, clearing negative energies and density that may be lodging there. You can use the image of a violet flame campfire, the flame of a gas burner or whatever visualization conveys to you the intensity and dynamism of a moving, living flame.

Send the violet flame through each chakra in turn, giving each affirmation in multiples of three as you see the violet flame clearing and purifying that chakra.

I AM a being of violet fire!
I AM the purity God desires!

My heart is a chakra of violet fire,
My heart is the purity God desires!

I AM a being of violet fire!
I AM the purity God desires!

My throat chakra is a wheel of violet fire,
My throat chakra is the purity God desires!

I AM a being of violet fire!
I AM the purity God desires!

Wanting to Be Loved

My solar plexus is a sun of violet fire,
My solar plexus is the purity God desires!

I AM a being of violet fire!
I AM the purity God desires!

My third eye is a center of violet fire,
My third eye is the purity God desires!

I AM a being of violet fire!
I AM the purity God desires!

My soul chakra is a sphere of violet fire,
My soul is the purity God desires!

I AM a being of violet fire!
I AM the purity God desires!

My crown chakra is a lotus of violet fire,
My crown chakra is the purity God desires!

I AM a being of violet fire!
I AM the purity God desires!

My base chakra is a fount of violet fire,
My base chakra is the purity God desires!

I AM a being of violet fire!
I AM the purity God desires!

The Resurrection Flame

Another spiritual exercise to help raise your energy and increase your light is based on the resurrection mantra of Jesus, "I AM the resurrection and the life."[1]

The resurrection is a resurgence of God's energy in our spiritual centers. Jesus was able to draw forth of the flame of resurrection from his I AM Presence and from the base-of-the-spine chakra to restore life to his own body in the ritual of the resurrection. Each of us can invoke this same flame for our own healing and the restoration of our physical body and our finer bodies to their inner design.

To begin, stand with your arms raised over your head. Imagine that you are directing the energy that is rising up the network of your chakras back to your I AM Presence.

See and feel the light within you as a mother-of-pearl softness bathing your body in a gentle glow. See the light surround every cell and atom of your body, becoming whiter and whiter. As the cells and atoms accelerate, they begin to spin—releasing the white light to clear and energize your body, mind and emotions.

As you hold this visualization, give the following affirmation aloud three times, nine times, or as many times as you wish.

**I AM, I AM, I AM the resurrection and the life
of every cell and atom of my four lower bodies
now made manifest!**

Feel the light and energy rising within you as you give this mantra, and experience the joy and lightness of the flame of the resurrection. It is particularly effective in raising and alleviating the buildup of excess energy around the lower chakras.

This affirmation can be used whenever you feel that the energy flow in some area of your life is blocked. Replace the words "every cell and atom of my four lower bodies" with the specific area of your life you want to rejuvenate. Many people use it for their finances: "I AM, I AM, I AM the resurrection and the life of my finances (3x), now made manifest in my hands and use today."

The "Hail Mary"

A third exercise for raising the light is one that has been used for hundreds of years, the giving of the "Hail Mary." The inner meaning of "Hail Mary" is "Hail Ma-Ray," or "Hail Mother Ray." This mantra is a salutation to the Universal Mother and also to the Mother light that is sealed in the base chakra. In the same way that yoga, mantra and meditation have been used in the East for the raising of the Kundalini, the "Hail Mary" is the spiritual exercise that has been given to those in the West for safely raising this energy.

This prayer is combined with the Lord's Prayer and other prayers and meditations in the ritual of the rosary. The rosary, then, is for the balance of the masculine and feminine polarity of being.

The New Age rosary has slightly different words for the Hail Mary, which affirm that we are sons and daughters of God (rather than that we are sinners) and asks the Blessed Mother to pray for us at the hour, not of our death, but "of our victory over sin, disease and death."

> Hail, Mary, full of grace.
>   The Lord is with thee.
> Blessed art thou among women
>   and blessed is the fruit of thy womb, Jesus.

Holy Mary, Mother of God,
Pray for us, sons and daughters of God,
Now and at the hour of our victory
Over sin, disease and death.

This prayer can be given as part of the rosary or it may be given alone as a mantra for the safe and gentle raising of the Mother light within.

Through this prayer, Mary has pledged to assist us in gaining our self-mastery. She has encouraged us to ask her to come into our lives, and she will assist us in the mastery of the Mother light or with any problem, great or small.

Heart, Head and Hand Decrees

The "Heart, Head and Hand Decrees" are simple mantras in verse form that contain keys to the stages of the spiritual path culminating in the ascension. These mantras also release the violet flame.

If you give these mantras aloud three times each or more every day, you will find that the energy that comes through them will assist you in fulfilling your divine plan, reuniting with your Higher Self and your twin flame, and fulfilling the requirements for the ascension. As you give them, know that many angels and masters in heaven are giving them with you.

Heart, Head and Hand Decrees

Violet Fire

Heart

See the violet flame in the center of your chest, around your heart and the heart chakra.

> Violet fire, thou love divine,
> Blaze within this heart of mine!
> Thou art mercy forever true,
> Keep me always in tune with you. (3x)

Head

See the violet flame through and around your head,
clearing the throat, third-eye and crown chakras.

> I AM light, thou Christ in me,
> Set my mind forever free;
> Violet fire, forever shine
> Deep within this mind of mine.
>
> God who gives my daily bread,
> With violet fire fill my head
> Till thy radiance heavenlike
> Makes my mind a mind of light. (3x)

Hand

See the violet flame passing through your hands, purify-
ing all of your actions and everyone and everything you
touch.

> I AM the hand of God in action,
> Gaining victory every day;
> My pure soul's great satisfaction
> Is to walk the Middle Way. (3x)

Tube of Light

See yourself standing in your tube of light, a cylinder of
white light that descends from your I AM Presence.

> Beloved I AM Presence bright,
> Round me seal your tube of light
> From ascended master flame
> Called forth now in God's own name.
> Let it keep my temple free
> From all discord sent to me.

I AM calling forth violet fire
To blaze and transmute all desire,
Keeping on in freedom's name
Till I AM one with the violet flame. (3x)

Forgiveness

Send violet-flame spheres from your heart to any situation that needs the light of forgiveness. Send them to those you need to forgive and to those who need to forgive you. See them as balls of flame with wings, traveling swiftly to their destination.

I AM forgiveness acting here,
Casting out all doubt and fear,
Setting men forever free
With wings of cosmic victory.

I AM calling in full power
For forgiveness every hour;
To all life in every place
I flood forth forgiving grace. (3x)

Supply

The highest symbol for abundance is gold, which represents not only the wealth of this world but also the spiritual gifts and graces that we need to fulfill our mission. As you give this mantra, see yourself bathed in the emerald-green light of healing and precipitation with gold coins descending from above into your upturned hands.

I AM free from fear and doubt,
Casting want and misery out,
Knowing now all good supply
Ever comes from realms on high.

Wanting to Be Loved

I AM the hand of God's own fortune
Flooding forth the treasures of light,
Now receiving full abundance
To supply each need of life. (3x)

Perfection

*See a sphere of blue flame of protection and divine
direction all around you, inspiring you with clarity in
decisions great and small.*

I AM life of God-direction,
Blaze thy light of truth in me.
Focus here all God's perfection,
From all discord set me free.

Make and keep me anchored ever
In the justice of thy plan—
I AM the Presence of perfection
Living the life of God in man! (3x)

Transfiguration

*See yourself literally setting aside old, worn-out gar-
ments, representing states of consciousness and elements
of the aura you want to leave behind. See in their place
new garments of light, with the light of the transfiguration all around you—a scintillating radiance containing
the white light and all of the seven rays.*

I AM changing all my garments,
Old ones for the bright new day;
With the sun of understanding
I AM shining all the way.

I AM light within, without;
I AM light is all about.
Fill me, free me, glorify me!
Seal me, heal me, purify me!
Until transfigured they describe me:
I AM shining like the Son,
I AM shining like the Sun! (3x)

Resurrection

See the mother-of-pearl light of the transfiguration accelerating so that the colors begin to merge into the white light.

I AM the flame of resurrection
Blazing God's pure light through me.
Now I AM raising every atom,
From every shadow I AM free.

I AM the light of God's full Presence,
I AM living ever free.
Now the flame of life eternal
Rises up to victory. (3x)

Ascension

See the white light of the ascension flame all around you, raising your whole body and consciousness into a higher dimension.

I AM ascension light,
Victory flowing free,
All of good won at last
For all eternity.

I AM light, all weights are gone.
Into the air I raise;
To all I pour with full God-power
My wondrous song of praise.

All hail! I AM the living Christ,
The ever-loving One.
Ascended now with full God-power,
I AM a blazing Sun! (3x)

These mantras are easy to memorize and you can give them anywhere. When they are given as a chant, the regular rhythm of the words adds its own power to the release. There is a momentum that builds and an intensification of light as you repeat them. As you give them on a regular basis, you may find that they naturally accelerate in speed and pitch as the light accelerates within you.

Prayer for the Protection of the Sacred Fire

The following prayer can assist you when you desire to conserve the light of the sacred fire in your spiritual centers and are faced with the pull of lesser desires. Give it in full voice with the assurance that help is always near.

I call in the name of my mighty I AM Presence and Holy Christ Self to the Divine Mother, to the heart of the Father-Mother God, beloved Alpha and Omega, and to the heart of the Christ.

I pray for the lawful fulfillment of the need of my soul for contact with the Divine Mother. I ask for the raising up and purifying of the energies of my chakras and for the transmutation of the cause and core of all misuse of the sacred fire.

I call for the binding of all forces that would intensify carnal desire. I ask for the fulfillment of every need of my soul and my I AM Presence through the heart chakra, and I ask for the marriage of my soul to my I AM Presence through my heart chakra.

According to God's holy will, let it be done. Amen.

Prayer for the Reunion
of Twin Flames

The Ascended Master El Morya speaks of the causes of the separation of twin flames and offers a prayer that may be given by those who seek reunion. Many people who have given this ritual have found that their prayer has been answered in wonderful ways.

> Understand that the highest and most perfect love begins with your individual expression of the heart, the expansion of that flame of love until all irritation is consumed and pride is not and you stand before your God truly worthy of whatever blessing can be given.
>
> Inasmuch as personal karma is the key factor separating twin flames and inasmuch as it is desirable that twin flames unite in service, the x factor that can make the difference is the entering in of one of the Ascended Masters ... to sponsor that union by pledging to take on the karma that does keep apart those souls. This sponsorship is like the sponsorship of the individual chela except it is the joint sponsorship of the twain.
>
> This, then, is a call you ought to include in your prayers. It is a call that says:

O God, I desire to perform the best service and to fulfill my inner vow with my twin flame. If it be that karma does separate us and therefore our service, I pray, let the LORD God set it aside for an hour and a year that we might show ourselves worthy, plow the straight furrow, enter into the service of our God and our country and of world freedom that together we may choose to balance that karma. And we do choose to do so, LORD God.

We pledge, then, no matter what may come, that if we be united, we will serve in harmony by the grace of God to first balance the karma taken on by an Ascended Master that that one need not carry for us the burden that is truly our own.

Thus having so said, it is important to record on paper in your own writing this prayer and whatever you have added to it with the date carefully inscribed and with your signature. You may insert it in the book of the Everlasting Gospel.

You must remind yourself to call to Archangel Michael to defend the highest encounter and to bind all impostors of your twin flame. For as soon as the desire is set and the sail is raised on your ship, the false hierarchy will send in those of attraction, of glamour or of heavy karma or even the initiators that come out of the depths of darkness posing as the Krishna, the holy one of God that is thine own.[2]

Angels of Protection

As El Morya explained in the previous quote, if you seek the reunion with your twin flame it is important to call for the protection of all that would oppose this. The following prayer and decree can be used for this purpose.

Begin with the opening prayer, then give the body of the decree aloud nine times or more. Send your love and gratitude to this great archangel for his presence and protection with you. See him with his sword of blue flame protecting you and your twin flame, cutting you free from all that would stand in the way of your highest love. Repeat the refrain after each verse.

Prayer and Decree to Archangel Michael
for the Protection of Twin Flames

In the name of my Mighty I AM Presence, I call now for the victory of my twin flame, for the cutting free of my twin flame by the power of the mighty blue flame and sword of Archangel Michael. Legions of Light, come into action now! And wherever my twin flame is, cut that one free. Cut me free. Cut us free now to fulfill the divine plan and attain union in the level of the Christ, in the level of our chakras. And if it be the will of God, draw us together in a lifetime of service. We thank you and accept it done this hour in full power according to God's will. Amen.

1. Lord Michael, Lord Michael,
        I call unto thee—
    Wield thy sword of blue flame
        And now cut me free!

Refrain: Blaze God-power, protection
            Now into my world,
        Thy banner of Faith
            Above me unfurl!

        Transcendent blue lightning
            Now flash through my soul,
        I AM by God's mercy
            Made radiant and whole!

2. Lord Michael, Lord Michael,
        I love thee, I do—
    With all thy great Faith
        My being imbue!

3. Lord Michael, Lord Michael
        And legions of blue—
    Come seal me, now keep me
        Faithful and true!

Coda: I AM with thy blue flame
            Now full-charged and blesst,
        I AM now in Michael's
            Blue-flame armor dressed! (3x)

And in full faith I consciously accept this manifest, manifest, manifest! (3x) right here and now with full power, eternally
sustained, all-powerfully active, ever expanding, and world enfolding until all are wholly ascended in the light and free!

Beloved I AM! Beloved I AM! Beloved I AM!

9
Eight Keys
for Raising
Your Energy

I n addition to prayer, decrees and spiritual techniques, there are practical steps that anyone can take to help with the problem of lack of flow of energy and the accumulation of energy in the lower chakras. Here are eight practical keys:

1. Pay attention to diet.

It can be very helpful to cut down on red meat, sugar, and rich, spicy or fatty foods, which tend to act as stimulants and focus more energy in the physical body. Many also find it helpful to refrain from dairy products.

A diet based on whole grains and vegetables with moderate amounts of proteins and other foods is not only healthy for the physical body, but also helps to bring balance to the mental, emotional and etheric bodies as well.

2. Balance the body with exercise.

Exercise is very important for the flow of the energies and the balance of the body. It helps to expand the heart and the lungs and assists in the control of the physical body and the flow of energy in the body.

After physical exercise such as walking, swimming or jogging, you can also sit and meditate on the third-eye chakra and feel the energies gently rise upon the spine. Activities such as hatha yoga and T'ai Chi are specifically designed for maintaining a healthy flow of energy in the body.

If there is an immediate issue with sexual energies, the old remedy of taking a cold shower actually works. It gives a certain shock to the body and alters the flow of circulation.

3. Stay away from alcohol and other drugs.
Apart from the negative effects drugs and alcohol have on the physical body and the spiritual centers, people often do things they later regret while under the influence of alcohol or other drugs.*

4. Avoid situations where you will be tempted.
While it seems obvious, simply avoiding temptation can be a good strategy. If a situation arises where you might have a problem, often all you have to do is simply leave the scene and be with other people.

Just saying no actually works. And if you know that you will be tempted ahead of time, avoid those situations.

It also helps to choose your friends wisely. Spend time with people walking a similar path rather than those who might draw you into situations that would make it more difficult for you to preserve your light and keep your commitments to yourself and your twin flame.

5. Be selective in what you watch and read.
Pornography in all forms is clearly something to avoid, since it is designed to stimulate sexual energies and to draw your

---

* One reason alcohol is such a problem in this regard is that it first affects the higher centers in the brain, the physical point of contact with our higher self. The lack of inhibition that people feel under the influence of alcohol is also a disconnection from the voice of conscience, the Holy Christ Self. For information about the spiritual aspects of drugs of all kinds, see my book *Wanting to Be Free: A Spiritual Perspective on Addiction and Recovery.*

energies to the lower chakras.* But many mainstream and even family-oriented movies and television shows these days have a lot of sexual content, either overt or through innuendo. When you watch them, it is almost impossible for your energies not to be drawn to the lower chakras.

Be selective. If something is showing that is going to lower your energies, fast forward, don't watch that movie, change the channel or turn off the TV. Observe what happens to your energies and make choices that will help you keep your energies where you want them to be.

6. Choose what you listen to.

Music is another factor that profoundly affects the flow of energy and light in the body. Music with sexual themes and lyrics has an obvious effect, but beyond this there is a science to music and its effects on the body.

The natural rhythm of the base-of-the-spine chakra is the 4/4 of the disciplined march beat. Music with a rock beat (a syncopated 4/4, where the stress is on the second and fourth beats of the measure) resonates with the base chakra and throws it off balance. Instead of the light rising through the chakras, this music draws the light downwards on the spine.

It is no coincidence that the era of the rise of rock music in the 1960s was also the time when free love became fashionable. Millions of young people listening to this new music had their energies focused in their lower chakras and did not know how to handle it. The sexual revolution was their way out.

---

* The easy access to pornography through the Internet has led to a widespread problem of pornography addiction, which has had devastating effects on many lives and relationships. For more about the addictive nature of pornography and the damage it causes, especially for young men, see http://yourbrainonporn.com. For spiritual techniques to overcome this and other addictions, see *Wanting to Be Free: A Spiritual Perspective on Addiction and Recovery.*

It is difficult to avoid the beat of rock music today, since it has become the soundtrack of so much of modern life. But if you can avoid listening to it when you have a choice, you will find that it is easier to deal with the energies of the base chakra and to raise the light. Classical music and the 3/4 time of the waltz (the natural rhythm of the physical heart and the heart chakra) help to raise the light.

7. Examine your desires and resolve your personal psychology. If you are having a problem that is of long standing and you can't seem to get a handle on it, especially if it is starting to feel like an addiction, it may be helpful to do some work on your psychology. Sometimes these issues arise from nonresolution with parents or other issues from childhood, and the help of a professional counselor can be of great assistance, especially when combined with spiritual work.

8. Develop a relationship with a saint or ascended master. Sometimes problems with the sacred fire arise from an underlying desire for wholeness that seeks fulfillment in a twin flame or soul mate. While waiting for the time when that one is at your side, choose a master or saint you feel close to—perhaps Jesus, Saint Francis or Krishna if you are a woman, Mother Mary or another female saint if you are a man, and find wholeness through a relationship with that one.

We can develop real relationships with the saints and masters by reading about their lives and teachings, praying to them and giving their decrees, having conversations with them, writing letters to them, and having their pictures in our homes. Like any other relationship, this will take some time and effort. It may seem like all the communication is all in one direction at the beginning, but over time you will feel the return current as a subtle energy and a sense of a real presence in your life.

Mother Teresa of Calcutta had such a relationship with Jesus. Someone once said to her, "Well, you know, it's easier for you. You're not married or in a relationship." "What do you mean? I am married," she said, showing the ring on her finger that signifies a nun's marriage to Jesus, "and he can be very difficult, too!"[1] A relationship with a saint or an ascended master can help to fulfill the inner need that we all have for a relationship with the other polarity of our inner being.

John is a man who is now in his thirties. He was sexually active in his late teens and early twenties but found it did not lead to satisfaction in his soul. He now uses these keys to gain a degree of mastery over his energies. He exercises regularly and says the rosary every day. He is careful about what shows he watches and keeps the remote handy if things get too steamy. John explains the changes he has seen in his life:

"I thought I could not live without sex, but at the same time I could not stand the roundabout of casual affairs that really did not mean anything. I stumbled across these keys and I applied them diligently, probably because I was desperate. Now I know my limits and I avoid situations where I know I will get into trouble.

"I am not ashamed to pray and to ask the angels for help when I need it. I feel that God will lead me to the right person when the time is right. In the meantime I am happy to wait for God's timing. And to tell the truth, although I never thought that I could say it, I now know that I am fine as I am."

10
The Highest Love

No, *the heart that has truly loved never forgets,*
  But as truly loves on to the close,
As the sunflower turns on her god when he sets,
  The same look which she turned when he rose!

THOMAS MOORE

A New Way

My conversations and counseling with teenagers and those of all ages lead me to believe that people really want to love and be loved. They seek the greater love, the perfect love, the person they are destined to be with in this life. Somehow, they still believe that this love of the beloved will carry them through all of life's trials and tests. Even while they acknowledge the value of the relative freedoms we have today, there is also a desire to return to some of the values of their parents' or grandparents' time, and there is a sense of sorrow at the disappearance of the traditional way of family life.

Teens are concerned that so many marriages end in divorce. Even though they are grateful that their own (often single) parents loved them and cared for them, they do not want to continue the current trend whereby half of all marriages end badly. They have survived their parents' divorces and want to follow a different path. Lauren Harper, a senior at the University of Georgia, said in an article in the *Atlanta Journal-Constitution*: "My friends want to find their soul mate and get married. They want a family and a career."[1]

But we can't just turn back the clock. We live in a world that is very different from that of our parents or grandparents, a time where seemingly anything goes. People today probably know more about sex than any generation in history, but do we know any more about love? How do we navigate through this new world, where the old rules no longer apply? Where are the signposts that point the way to real love?

Perhaps what is needed is a new way of looking at love, sex and relationships—through an understanding of energy, of flow, of spiritual principles. With this awareness, we can make choices based not on tradition or fear or rules or social pressure, but on true love and enlightenment. Isn't this what a new age should be all about?

The principles in this book have helped young people and those of all ages to gain mastery in their spiritual centers and to raise their light from the base to the crown. They have found greater creativity and fulfillment in life. A spiritual understanding of love and relationships has enabled them to have the courage and the faith to wait for a higher love.

For many, this path has been the means of finding the loving relationship they were seeking, the One they were destined to be with. For others, it has also been the key to finding the love that is within and communion with their Higher Self. For myself and my husband, Peter, it has been both of these things.

The relationships in our lives serve their highest purpose when they are a means for us to grow in love, to learn to give and receive more love. And as we express a greater love, we actually become more of God—for God is love. And this is perhaps the greatest secret of love.

Sometimes people have the sense that love is like a valuable commodity, something we must search for, discover. But love is not an object, but an action; not a noun, but a verb.

If we are trying to find this thing called "love," we may be disappointed. We may not find it. It may not live up to our expectations. If we seek instead to love, this is always possible. We can always start with loving God, our Higher Self and the Higher Self of our twin flame—wherever that one may be in Spirit or in matter.

So rather trying to find the right relationship as the goal, think about a focus on serving others. As we serve and give of ourselves, we will meet all sorts of wonderful people who also seek to serve. And selflessness will draw us to a higher love.

As we send more love out into the world, then love will also return to us in greater measure. The more we love, the more we will meet loving people. This is universal law. How this love will return, we may not be able to foresee.

It may be through the love of God that becomes a very tangible presence with us. It may be through an inner connection with our twin flame that lends a strength and joy to all that we do. It may be through the person of the twin flame or soul mate we meet as a companion for our life's journey. It may be through the opportunity to balance karma and be free of a burden that has weighed on us for many lifetimes.

Whatever our destined path, sharing our love will bring us closer to the goal. This is the path that all of the great saints and mystics, the avatars of East and West, have taught.

Love is the key to the solution of every problem. Love is the key that opens every door. The only way to become an adept or a master, to win our ascension, is through love. Strive to share the love that you seek, and love will return to you abundantly.

Love is long-suffering, love is kind.
Love does not envy, it does not boast,
it is not proud.
Love is not rude, it is not self-centered.
Love is not easily angered.
Love forgives and does not remember
the wrongs of others.
Love does not rejoice in evil, but rejoices
in the truth.
Love never gives up, always believes,
always hopes, always perseveres.
Love endures forever.

SAINT PAUL

Acknowledgments

I n the years of my pursuing the spiritual path with Elizabeth Clare Prophet, I had the opportunity to be present in many sessions as she provided teaching and counseling to people about twin flames, soul mates and relationships. In these sessions I saw a great depth of spiritual insight and a great love for the souls with whom she came in contact. I also saw her profound understanding of the human condition and her ability to bring the soul to a higher place in consciousness. The teachings were often life-changing.

I have long hoped to see those teachings on love, sex and relationships reach a wider audience, and that is the purpose of this book. Mrs. Prophet's teachings on soul mates, twin flames, and karmic relationships are the core of the message. Some of the most important original sources are listed in the section of Additional Resources at the end of this book. To the framework of these concepts I have added insights gained from my own experience and counseling and many stories of people I have known that illustrate how these concepts have applied in the real world.

In some of these case studies, the individuals have shared intuitive insights about their past lives or the spiritual nature of their relationships. I cannot personally confirm or deny the accuracy of these insights, but I share them here because they were often key elements of these individuals' own understanding of their relationships. Many of the stories are archetypal, and there are lessons we might all learn from them.

I would like to express my deep gratitude to Mrs. Prophet and her husband Mark for their role as pioneers of spirituality and for bringing these concepts to the world. I would also like to thank Summit University Press for permission to draw from Mrs. Prophet's teachings in compiling this book.

My thanks go to Marilyn Barrick, a spiritual psychologist of many years' experience, who reviewed an early draft of the manuscript, offered insights into the psychology of love and relationships, and provided some of the case studies. Thanks also to Ralph and Lucille Yaney for sharing the fruit of their many years practice as therapists and counselors, and particularly the concepts in the section "Keeping It Real."

Finally, I would like to thank the many young people who reviewed this book in manuscript form, offered advice and insights into the challenges of relationships today, and encouraged me to see this project through to completion.

Notes

INTRODUCTION

1. **Bitter in the belly:** Rev. 10:10.

CHAPTER 1

Opening quote: Thomas Merton, *Love and Living* (San Diego, Calif.: Harcourt, 1985), p. 27.

1. **There lived by the sea:** Elizabeth Clare Prophet, *Soul Mates and Twin Flames* (Gardiner, Mont.: Summit University Press, 1999), pp. 69–71.

2. Prayer adapted from *Soul Mates and Twin Flames*, p. 52.

3. **The violet flame comes forth:** El Morya, *The Chela and the Path* (Gardiner, Mont.: Summit University Press, 1976), p. 47.

4. **I AM THAT I AM:** Exod. 3:14, 15.

CHAPTER 2

Opening quote: Chamuel and Charity, *Pearls of Wisdom*, vol. 29, no. 26.

1. **Divine Love always has met:** Mary Baker Eddy, *Science and Health with Key to the Scriptures*, p. 494.

2. **Chariot of fire:** 2 Kings 2:11; **walked with God:** Gen. 5:24.

3. **A great multitude:** Rev. 7:9.

4. **Wedding garment:** Matt. 22:11–12.

CHAPTER 3

Opening quote: *Soul Mates and Twin Flames*, p. 62.

1. **Unequally yoked:** 2 Cor. 6:14.

2. **Sufficient unto the day is the evil thereof:** Matt. 6:34.

3. **Marriage requires a commitment:** Elizabeth Clare Prophet, August 10, 1990; June 6, 1986.

4. **Sometimes people don't marry:** Elizabeth Clare Prophet, June 6, 1986.

5. **Those who are the adherents:** Omri-Tas, "I Will Keep the Vow," *Pearls of Wisdom*, vol. 49, no. 1, January 1, 2006.

6. **Peter was married:** Matt. 8:14; Mark 1:30; Luke 4:38; **bishops should be married:** I Tim. 3:2–4.

7. **The first decrees by church councils on priestly celibacy** were from the Council of Elvira (A.D. 306) and the Council of Nicea (A.D. 325).

8. **Thy Maker is thine husband:** Isa. 54:5.

CHAPTER 4

Opening quote: Letter from Henry David Thoreau to Harrison Blake, September 1852, in *The Writings of Henry David Thoreau* (Boston: Houghton Mifflin, 1906), vol. 6.

1. One aspect of the **psychological/spiritual consequences of early promiscuity** is seen in a study of more than 7,000 high-school females published by the Rutgers School of Public Health in 2013, which stated: "The prevalence of sadness, suicide ideation, suicide plans and suicide attempts increased with the number of sexual partners across all racial/ethnic groups." Tyree Oredein, "The Relationship between Multiple Sexual Partners and Mental Health in Adolescent Females," *Journal of Community Medicine & Health Education*, 3:256. doi: 10.4172/2161-0711.1000256

2. For more about **fallen angels,** see Elizabeth Clare Prophet, *Fallen Angels and the Origins of Evil* (Gardiner, Mont.: Summit University Press, 2000).

3. **You can't help it if a bird lands on your head:** El Morya, quoted in Mark L. Prophet and Elizabeth Clare Prophet, *Lost Teachings on Your Higher Self* (Gardiner, Mont.: Summit University Press, 2005), p. 11.

4. For more information about the **retreats of the masters** on the etheric plane, see Mark L. Prophet and Elizabeth Clare Prophet, *The Masters and Their Retreats* (Gardiner, Mont.: Summit University Press, 2003).

5. **Male and female created he them:** Gen. 1:1, 26, 27.

6. *Sushumna, ida* and *pingala*: Sanskrit terms for currents of wisdom, power and love emanating from the white-fire core of the base-of-the-spine chakra and which flow in and around the spinal altar.

7. Mark L. Prophet and Elizabeth Clare Prophet, *The Path to Attainment* (Gardiner, Mont.: Summit University Press, 2008), pp. 46–47.

8. An increasing body of research by social scientists is showing that **sexual orientation is much more fluid than previously believed.** They are finding that it is not uncommon for people identifying as exclusively homosexual at one period in their life to enter into a heterosexual relationship at a later time. See, for example, Lisa M. Diamond, *Sexual Fluidity: Understanding Women's Love and Desire* (Cambridge, Mass.: Harvard University Press, 2009).

9. **The prince of this world:** John 14:30.

CHAPTER 5

Opening quote: Chamuel and Charity, *Pearls of Wisdom*, vol. 29, no. 26.

1. **If you can't be with the one you love:** Stephen Stills, "Love the One You're With."

2. **Seek ye first the kingdom of God:** Matt. 6:33 (emphasis added).

3. **Letting God write your love story:** Eric Ludy and Leslie Ludy, *When God Writes Your Love Story: The Ultimate Guide to Guy/Girl Relationships* (Sisters, Ore.: Multnomah Publishers, 2004).

4. The story of **Jesus' journey to the East** is told in ancient Pali texts found in the nineteenth century in Ladakh. See Elizabeth Clare Prophet, *The Lost Years of Jesus* (Gardiner, Mont.: Summit University Press, 1987).

5. **We picture lovers:** C. S. Lewis, *The Four Loves* (New York: Harcourt, 1991), p. 66.

Notes

6. **One young man's strategy:** Joshua Harris, *I Kissed Dating Goodbye* (Colorado Springs: Multnomah Books, 1997), p. 80.
7. **The very condition:** Lewis, *The Four Loves*, p. 66.
8. **All love that has not:** Ella Wheeler Wilcox, "Upon the Sand."
9. **Do not arouse:** Song of Solomon 8:4 (New International Version).
10. **Don't marry unless:** Sue Patton Thoele, *Heart Centered Marriage: Fulfilling Our Natural Desire for Sacred Partnership* (Berkeley, Calif.: Conari Press, 1996).
11. **Be not unequally yoked:** 2 Cor. 6:14.
12. These two questions along with the concepts in this section are drawn from a lecture by Elizabeth Clare Prophet, "Marriage as an Initiation on the Path," October 7, 1976.

CHAPTER 6

Opening quote: Chamuel and Charity, *Pearls of Wisdom*, vol. 29, no 20.

1. "Marriage as an Initiation on the Path."
2. *Soul Mates and Twin Flames,* pp. 100–02.
3. **The Father worketh hitherto:** John 5:17.
4. **Give your hearts:** Kahlil Gibran, *The Prophet* (New York: Alfred A. Knopf, 1923), p. 16.
5. Elizabeth Clare Prophet, *Vials of the Seven Last Plagues* (Gardiner, Mont.: Summit University Press, 2004), pp. 35–37.

CHAPTER 7

Opening quote: Matt. 19:6.

1. "And the LORD God caused a deep sleep to fall upon Adam, and he slept: and he took one of his ribs, and closed up the flesh instead thereof; And the rib, which the LORD God had taken from man, made he a woman, and brought her unto the man. And Adam said, This is now bone of my bones, and flesh of my flesh: she shall be called Woman, because she was taken out of Man" (Gen. 1:21–22).
2. **What therefore God hath joined together:** Matt. 19:6.

CHAPTER 8

Opening quote: Elizabeth Clare Prophet, November 20, 1980.

1. **I AM the resurrection and the life:** John 11:25.
2. El Morya, *Pearls of Wisdom*, vol. 28, no. 23, August 18, 1985.

CHAPTER 9

1. **Mother Teresa:** Jack Kornfield, in Fred Eppsteiner, ed., *The Path of Compassion: Writing on Socially Engaged Buddhism* (Berkeley: Parallax Press, 1988), p. 27.

CHAPTER 10

1. **My friends want:** Lauren Harper, "Younger Generation Shuns Divorce," *The Atlanta Journal-Constitution*, October 22, 2002.

Additional Resources

The following releases by Elizabeth Clare Prophet give more depth on many of the concepts covered in this book. They are available from

The Summit Lighthouse
63 Summit Way, Gardiner, MT 59030
+1 (406) 848-9500
www.SummitLighthouse.org
TSLinfo@TSL.org

Audio and video recordings:
June 15, 1974, "Your Marriage Made in Heaven"
June 15, 1974, "Your Marriage Made on Earth"
June 15, 1974, "Karma, Reincarnation and the Family"
October 11, 1975, "Man and Woman in Transition"
October 7, 1976, "Marriage as an Initiation on the Path"
July 3, 1977, "Twin Flames in Love"
April 21, 1978, "Twin Flames in Love"
April 22, 1978, "Twin Flames in Love in the Circle of
    Oneness"
July 5, 1982, lecture on twin flames
July 5, 1982, lecture on soul mates; questions and answers
July 5, 1985, questions and answers on twin flames
November 17, 1985, questions and answers on twin flames

June 8, 1986, "Twin Flames in the Aquarian Age"
May 20, 1989, "The Divine Plan of Twin Flames"
Twin Flames in Love (audio, includes the 1978 lectures above)
Twin Flames in Love (video, includes the July 5, 1982, lecture
    on twin flames)

Audio and video recordings on related topics:

The Power of Music to Create or Destroy (explanation of the
    spiritual effects of music; video)
Chakra Meditations and the Science of the Spoken Word
    (audio)
A Child's Rosary to Mother Mary (audio)

Books on relationships:

Soul Mates and Twin Flames
The Path to Attainment, chapter 1, "Twin Rays"

Books on related topics:

Violet Flame to Heal Body, Mind and Soul
The Science of the Spoken Word
How to Work with Angels

Also available from Summit University Press:

*Sacred Psychology of Love: The Quest for Relationships That
    Unite Heart and Soul*, by Marilyn C. Barrick